To

Steve &

w/

Warmest regards,

WB + Ann

Carraway

TESTIMONIALS

Anything that Bill Carraway writes I want to read and reread because during, the 45 years of our friendship, I've found him to be forthright and truthful. What he believes he practices, and he works diligently to achieve his goals.

His positive attitude and approach are inspiring. He exudes a genuine joy which neither circumstances nor man can sway.

WB is a man of conviction, concern, and compassion. He preaches sound doctrine with untiring determination and unswerving devotion to the Lord Jesus Christ.

I have found him to be completely dedicated to the Son of God, thoroughly saturated with the Word of God, and fully activated by the Spirit of God!

Thomas B. Guinn, Chattanooga, TN

I've known Bill Carraway for 52 years--as a shipmate, preacher, and friend. His fidelity to solid mores, along with refusing to dillydally with truth, has been refreshing in a day of spiritual and moral torpidity.

Bill did not choose the ministry; it was selected for him. But he stands tall and true in his profession of 50 years, adamantly refusing to compromise biblical truth, which he has studied arduously. I'm glad to call him "friend."

Wayne Dandridge, Hillsboro, TX

OTHER BOOKS BY BAC PUBLICATIONS

A Call to Faith & Morality, by W. B. Carraway, 1993

Daughter of Destiny, by Carlene Howell, 1995

Blood's Thicker than Prejudice, by Letha Smith, 1996

ABOUT BAC PUBLICATIONS

This publishing company is merely an extension of a gospel ministry that began in 1946, forty-five years of which were spent in the pastorate among fourteen churches. W. B. was ordained September 6, 1946, by the Farley Street Baptist Church, Waxahachie, Texas.

Upon retirement June 1, 1991, Carraway began fulfilling a longtime dream--that of writing/publishing--by registering BAC Publications as a sole proprietorship business with the Comptroller of Texas, November 1, 1992.

All typesetting for BAC books, except cover copy, is done on a LASER 386 SX computer by the company's president. Then the completed camera-ready copy is sent to a book manufacturer for binding.

DO YOU HAVE A STORY TO TELL?

Not every writer is money-motivated only. Many write to share with and help their fellow-man. Infact, they feel that such is not only an opportunity but an obligation to God.

Why don't you write your story, even if it is hand-written, and let BAC Publications put it in book form for circulation. It's easier to do than you might think!

BASIC CHRISTIANITY

A STUDY & REPORT
FROM INSIDE THE CHURCH

W. B. Carraway

BAC PUBLICATIONS
7200 Preston, # 1213
Plano, Tx 75024-3224
(Dallas Metroplex)

Graphics/Editing

Camera-ready copy for this book's cover is the work of Joe Germann, Winnsboro, Texas. Judy King, Houston, Texas, gave editorial assistance.

LCCN: 96-84257
ISBN: 0-9633855-3-4

Published by
BAC Publications
P.O. Box 963
Winnsboro, Texas 75494

Printed in
the United States
of America

CONTENTS

MEET THE AUTHOR

W. B. Carraway, author; Anna Florence Carraway, wife; and Meghan E. McDermott, granddaughter.

INTRODUCTION

Homer's epic poem, *The Odyssey*, intrigues me. What a challenging, interesting, and difficult journey Odysseus, king of Ithaca, had in his ten-year effort to get home to Penelope, his wife, after the Trojan War. However, he is not the only person who (in life) experienced an odyssey (a long series of wanderings filled with notable experiences, hardships, challenges, and realizations). Most of us have! Though we did not request life, we accept it with gratitude, and launch an earnest effort to find our niche therein. Having found our *summun bonum* (chief good), we pursue with enthusiasm and dedication our prescribed journey, prayerfully hoping for the best. But, realistically, we prepare for the worst--should it come. Therefore, we have experienced an odyssey and have an interesting story to tell. What a shame for such an account to die with the deceased rather than being recorded for enjoyment and learning.

Looking over the seventy years of my odyssey, I find it interestingly filled with wonder, excitement, peace, joy, victories, beautiful associations with worthy people, reward, and awards, but to tell it as it really was, I must confess that there was another side too. Some of my journey has entailed boredom, mistakes, consternation, sadness, turbulence, despondency, defeat, betrayal, revulsion, and bewilderment. There have been many and varied antagonists (people, natural events, mysterious occurrences) I have had to fight as did Odysseus, but I've eventually survived to continue my journey homeward to heaven, the very thought of which gives me an inside glow.

MY ANCHOR

How have I made it thus far and how do I plan to make it back to my first love (not Penelope but Jesus)? I will do so because I know God and I also know, in those words of the Apostle John, that "greater is he that is in you, than he that is in the world" (I John 4:4). As the media jars and saddens my heart with its daily reports of rapes, murders, embezzlements, robberies, and many other kinds of evil, I know what has kept me from doing those dastardly deeds-- God and His effect of inner strength and prohibiting morals. I admit, "But for the grace of God, there go I!"

A PRICE TO PAY

Each recipient of mysterious and majestical existence has a life to live, a mission to fulfill, and a record to leave behind. Martin Luther risked his life in the defense of biblical truth and human dignity. Dietrich Bonhoeffer, the young Lutheran pastor in Germany, died on the Nazi gallows at Flossenberg Concentration Camp, April 9, 1945, rather than be passive toward Nazi atrocities. I believe if I had sold out to humans and humanism, I could have been the darling of two denominations. But as Blaise Pascal said, "When the heart finds God, it dedicates the recipient to a lifetime of resisting error."

WHY?

This book was written because I was compelled to write it. Had I not, I couldn't look my God in the face when I meet Him soon in eternity. Hebrews 9:27 tells us that each of us must die and face the judgment.

Conviction and responsibleness demand my leaving this inside information to posterity. "If a tree falls in the forest, and there's no one to hear it, does it make a sound?" In that same vein, allow me to ask: Is a book a book if no one reads it?

Regardless, none can know my story unless I publish it. It's my obligation to put it out; it is the duty of others to take it in. I cannot do both.

Therefore, this is the account of a born-again and committed child of God. Such a daring one will be shot from a double-barreled gun--the churchy world and the worldly church.

QUESTION AT YOUR OWN PERIL

I was pastoring my second ▮▮▮▮▮▮▮▮▮ church when two denominational leaders--guests of our church that day for the groundbreaking for a new building--were waiting in my office before the morning service. They repeatedly agreed that ▮▮▮▮▮▮▮▮▮ were doing great things and experiencing phenomenal success. Their remarks showed no sign of concern or caution, just elation over progress. I would guess that both of them had sore backs that night from the patting each was giving the other.

Finally I spoke up to say, "But with the program and advances, let us be sure that we stay with God and His Word." I will never forget the look on each face as it jerked to attention and in the direction of the other! I could have raked their eyeballs off their faces with a stick. There was no room in their jubilation for a hesitant or negative step as their steam-rolling Juggernaut roared through hamlets and cities making a big show in the flesh and becoming the largest Protestant denomination in the world! They, and their ilk, had no place in their churches for those who were not blindly aboard the bandwagon they were steering. The date was 1955 and both men are dead, but that which they praised that Lord's Day races on in filling the churches with the world, calling it evangelism and kingdom growth. But my speaking up was the kiss of death in the ███████████████████. And it will also be yours.

The denomination those two men were lauding honored numbers in reference to annual additions to the church, the average Sunday School attendance, the size of the church, and the amount of money raised and given, especially to denominational causes. (This assertion is easy to substantiate.) In other words, the emphasis was on "counting nickels and noses." Such is not biblical criteria for greatness in the kingdom of God; it is the world's standard.

I was astounded to witness the honoring of the "spectacle for the eyes," without question or investigation as to its authenticity, with write-ups in denominational periodicals and speaking invitations at denominational meetings. Those bereft of spiritual vision and biblical conviction sold their birthright for this mess of worldly pottage and joined the charade full sail for the reward of man rather than the approbation of God. When a person of God with a Holy Spirit-indwelt heart went to hear these empty wagons rattle at conventions, the listener was flabbergasted. Nothing worth hearing was coming forth! Consequently, the discerning hearer left disappointed.

THE SITUATION ANALYZED

What was the success secret of these man-made superstars building megachurches? Cheating! They were not following godly and biblical rules. God's way of requiring a complete and intelligent surrender to the Lordship of Christ before one was ready to be a part of the church was too slow for these pretending opportunists, so they just handled it themselves--filling the churches with worldly-minded people. These empty-hearted members would--in time--destroy any semblance of spirituality and orthodoxy there.

These cheating, Teflon luminaries were also using cheap, unworthy methods to build these (empty of heart) monstrosities such as pastor adoration and competition with the largest church in the community to surpass it in attendance and size. I witnessed a blatantly bold demonstration of this from the pastorate already mentioned. The nearby so-called church became the largest one (numerically) in its town. The (pathetic) pastor grabbed a larger (much larger) church in another state, where finally a lawyer-member published a 485-page book on this preacher's alleged infidelity and unorthodoxy. The church from which this great doctor (a seminary dropout) sprang has had two horrendous splits since he left and is of no consequence in its community today, so I'm told.

DENOMINATIONAL DECLINE

This denomination (and all others with which I am personally acquainted) has turned the churches into cafeterias (food and drink at most of its meetings), social clubs (fun and games galore), entertainment centers (with jazzy type music performances in the place of worship, followed by loud and long clapping), and cliques (meaning some won't associate with some--denying the body nature of the church). A born-again, Spirit-filled person can plainly see "Ichabod" above the door, i. e., "God's glory has departed." Oh, yes, the people are there, but the Spirit, sanction, and power of God are not. The big demonstration that's put on in the services is of man, not God.

A VISIT

I was visited one evening at home by a staff member and lay member of a sizeable church (for that community) with which I had once been associated and asked why I wasn't attending. I replied that I didn't feel comfortable in the church anymore, one reason for which was the wearing of walking shorts by a rather large contingent of young people right there in the church. The staffer said, "We don't like it either, but we're afraid if we say anything against it, we'll lose them." I responded, "You can't lose them because you don't have 'em; they've got you!"

Current churches are more and more having fewer and fewer rules and the ones existing are not enforced. Unenforced rules are no rules. This fact is destroying the local expression of the church. How true the saying, "All that good men have to do to be ruled by evil men is nothing."

THE NAZIS

I watch and read everything I can find on Nazi Germany. What a holocaust! Yet the people of that country allowed it. A parallel was the Japanese move to destroy and be destroyed in the bombing of Pearl Harbor, yet many of the citizens condoned it. Can we, dare we, who have those two object lessons embedded in our minds as to the cost of passiveness in reference to evil, let destruction and collapse come to America? That's exactly what the present trend of no involvement is doing. Let us rise up as one now and change the present dangerous and destructive course of our society.

The late M. R. De Hann of Grand Rapids, Michigan, in his book, *Chemistry of the Blood* (Zondervan, 1943), said in discussing a controversial practice, "I am going to give you a verse that will be unpopular with many of you, but I am not aiming to be popular with you; I have one desire: that I may be popular with Him who sent me to preach the Gospel!" Amen.

One highly regarded person in today's self-publishing world says, in print, that he thinks little of front matter in a book because very few read it. Respectfully, I say that he doesn't speak for me; I read every word of it from each book I peruse. It is my prayer that you have read this introduction because what follows will make more sense.

Finally, this is my story. I do not plan to write it again but to address other important subjects. May my mistakes and failures calm others in informing them they are not the only erring ones and also that God forgives and reinstates sinners. My sincere desire is that God's realness to me may be experienced by each person who reads this, my personal report. May my God of guidance, motivation, and restraint be allowed into the lives of all with whom I am allowed to share this study and memoir.

INTRODUCTION

What does it cost to let God into your life? Not much--just your whole being! The Bible and experience teach that one does not become a child of God and citizen of heaven without an all-out surrender of the total self to God. The virus now filling theology and the churches of "Come as you are; remain as you were!" is heretical and lethal--to the soul and to the church. It is not only unbiblical, it's nonsense.

Are the benefits worth the cost? Definitely--no ifs, ands, or buts about it! Specifically, what is the compensation? It is the four Ps: The **peace** of assurance, the **promise** of eternal life by One, who never has and never will break His promise, the **power** of self-discipline to enthrone the right and expel the wrong from one's life, and **permission** (hope) of leaving Planet Earth for a heavenly world.

W. B. Carraway

COMMENCEMENT

And just where does basic Christianity commence? It begins with our introduction to and discovery of the Bible, a
collection of sacred writings claiming for themselves divine
inspiration. This book, as earth's inhabitants now have it, is
actually an amassment of sixty-six books under one cover.
It is divided into two sections, the Old Testament and the
New Testament, with a gaping hole between the two. That
gap is 400 years wide!

Believe it or not, the space between Malachi, the concluding book of the Old Testament, and Matthew, the opening
book of the New Testament, is 400 years. During this
interbiblical period, no prophet of God walked the earth.
That is to say that there was no fresh-from-heaven word
for the earth's population. They had to do with what they
had.

When does this gradual introduction to the Bible first
occur in one's life? There is no set, universal time. For
those of Christian parentage, it begins early--in the home
and in the church. It may be later--much later--in life when
those of non-Christian birth have a precise impression of
the Bible and its social significance.

Whatever the reason, humankind reacts individually and
differently to the Bible. Some accept its authenticity and

plunge into the lifelong adventure of exploring it. Others, while not denying its claims or the assertion of adherents, never concern themselves with learning its contents or following its dictates. Then there are those, perhaps the majority, who give the Bible no credibility whatsoever. They neither read it, nor do they follow its teachings, as illustrated by the statement of a prominent and popular person in Texas. He said in one of his books, "I have no sense of religion; I'm not concerned whether there is a deity or not. I make no efforts to proselytize and I have resisted all attempts at being proselytized. The metaphysics of religion I understand, but reject." Those who subscribe to such a philosophy are legion and have predesigned their tombstone to be engraved with these words: "I did it my way." I wonder if they ever heard the words written in Proverbs 14:12: "There is a way which seemeth right unto a man, but the end thereof are the ways of death."

THE BIBLE'S MESSAGE

But read or unread, what is the message, in a nutshell, of this book called the Bible? Its essence never fades or vanishes; it is always there for all generations. What does it say?

"In the beginning God created the heaven and the earth" (Genesis 1:1). These two objects are seen by all with eyesight, who explain the phenomenon to those without it. And when any of them wonder how it all came to be, the biblical answer is as good a one as they'll ever hear. Now comes our next question: "But how did humankind become a part of this planet?" It, too, is easily answered from the Word of God.

"And God said, Let us make man in our image, after our likeness: and let them have dominion over the fish of the sea, and over the fowl of the air, and over the cattle, and over all the earth, and over every creeping thing that creepeth upon the earth. So God created man in his own image, in the image of God created he him; male and female created he them. And God blessed them, and God said unto them, Be fruitful, and multiply, and replenish the earth, and subdue it: and have dominion over the fish of the sea, and over the fowl of the air, and over every living thing that moveth upon the earth" (Genesis 1: 26-28).

A SPECIAL PEOPLE

And when the God-commanded multiplying reached a certain point, the Eternal One called Abraham (then Abram) from Ur of the Chaldees, to leave his country and head for another that the Lord would show him. Here he would start a unique segment of a growing population to be God's special people--missionaries to the rest.

This chosen race left its land and was in Egypt for 400 years. They, some seventy strong, began their stay as favored people; they departed it (one million in number) as abused slaves. Why did their status change? The pharaoh reigning when they entered was their friend because one of their very own (Joseph) had been his benefactor, but in time, a certain pharaoh ascended the throne who knew nothing about Joseph and the Israelites. Instead of seeing these foreigners as an asset, he considered them a detriment and a threat. Consequently, a persecution program was formulated to afflict and weaken them, causing the tortured to cry unto God for deliverance. God heard their

3

plea and raised up their deliverer in the midst of both friend and foe. Not one to bypass nature's laws, God took the necessary time to prepare Moses for the stringent assignment--forty years in a palace, followed by forty years in the desert. When the eighty years of training were completed, God's man was sent to lead God's crushed people back to where they came from--Canaan's land.

Inexcusable Disrespect

When one has spent 50 years feasting on the spiritual and moral diet of the Word of God, biblical applications will automatically be made to various behavioristic patterns. The verse just referred to has often come to my mind of late, viz., "Now there arose up a new king over Egypt, which knew not Joseph" (Exodus 1:8).

There is a deluge of disrespect toward the elders by the baby boomers. And, sorry to say, the ministerial leaders of today are leading the parade in this spectacle of ethical mistreatment. Truly, there has arisen a new class of leadership (?) that knows not Joseph! That class, however, is either ignoring or rewriting the Bible.

God's Word exhorts us to "rise up before the hoary (gray or white) head, and honour the face of the old man, and fear thy God: I am the Lord" (Leviticus 19:32). "The hoary head is a crown of glory, if it be found in the way of righteousness" (Proverbs 16:31).

As a youngster, I was taught to respect, even admire, older people. One of the great joys of my ministerial life of fifty years has been getting with older saints of God. Their wisdom sharpens my mind; their knowledge of God and the spiritual thrills and strengthens my soul. Realizing that "tribulation worketh patience; and patience, experience; and experience, hope" (Romans 5:3-4), I've been "thrice and four times blessed" by their voice of experience. And I've seriously pondered their input on the subjects we've discussed.

Recently, some members of a former pastorate insistently invited my wife and me to a service in which a member of their family was participating. This was a pastorate of pleasant reflections where God blessed and the people responded graciously. I knew the young pastor and he knew me, yet I was completely ignored by him in the service, not even being invited to pray one of the two prayers he prayed. I could never treat a fellow preacher and former pastor like that in a place where I had the honor of serving my Lord.

On the Brink of Canaan

The shorter route from Egypt to Canaan was a ten-day journey, but Moses did not take the northern road; he, under God's direction no doubt, chose the longer (much longer) route. Forty years lay between their Egypt and their Canaan, yet they were not barren years. Time was essential in getting Israel ready for its new home. Multitudinous laws of guidance, including the Decalogue, were God-given. The establishment of a place of worship (the Tabernacle) was authorized and its details prescribed. Battles were fought, miracle provisions were supplied repeatedly, punishment for rebellious disobedience was meted out, and vital lessons of survival (under the wings of the Almighty) were filed for future use. They were forty years in doing it, but the emigres finally reached their destination. However, there was a regrettable exception to their occupying their new home--their beloved leader couldn't accompany them. Earlier, Moses had disobeyed God, which is a dangerous thing for even a Moses to do. The Israelites, nearing their entrance into Canaan, stopped at Kadesh, where Miriam, the sister of Moses, died and was buried. Due to the barrenness of the area, the people blamed and berated Moses. He and Aaron sought counsel from God at the Tabernacle, where Moses was instructed to speak water from a rock that was there. Returning from the meeting with Jehovah, Moses gathered the people before the rock, but instead of speaking to the rock, the harassed leader struck it twice with his rod. An abundance of water flowed forth, enough for all the people and their cattle, but Moses was in trouble. He was charged by God with rebellion and disobedience. His sentence? He would stand on Mount Nebo of the Pisgah range in Moab, immediately east of the Jordan River and Jericho, and view the land of promise, but he would not be allowed to enter it.

Even though this beloved one of God begged for a second chance (to obey God at all times in all things) and the exhilaration of entering the long-sought-for land, his request was emphatically denied. Moses died on Mount Nebo, but his body was never found. I've heard two possible explanations. Some believe Moses was translated to heaven since he later appeared with Jesus on the Mountain of Transfiguration. Others, referring to Jude, verse 9, believe Satan battled with God over the body of Moses that it might be preserved, inducing idolatry on the part of the children of Israel. Of course, if this view be worthy, God won the skirmish, as He did the first one (Isaiah 14:12-15 and Ezekiel 28:12-19) and did with the bone of contention as He willed.

God Demands Obedience

God's treatment of Moses, in this instance, may seem to us severe, but our Sovereign had then/has now a point to make: He is to be unequivocally obeyed in every instruction given. He commands us primarily through the scriptures, which He took a long time to write through human instrumentality. He expects every precept to be not only kept, but executed to the fullest degree.

Moses made a big mistake by shifting the emphasis of the occasion from obedience to God to venting his frustration on the "rebels," as he called them. He lost his cool; he allowed his lower (worldly) self to take control of his behavior. How can we prevent this? One pungent answer will suffice: "Walk in the Spirit, and ye shall not fulfil the lust of the flesh" (Galatians 5:16). In order to be champions for Christ, we must starve our worldly-mindedness (carnality) while feeding our spiritual-mindedness. Our obsession (motivation) is God, our guidebook is the Bible, and our exercise is living life--in every category--as He has instructed.

God's Word dictates our lifestyle. We are to do our work six days a week, but the seventh day is to be kept holy unto God. This means going to church, resting, and thinking of our Lord while refraining from secular work and our own (fleshly) pleasure. It grieves a genuine child of God to witness today how the self-lovers, instead of God-lovers,

7

violate this request, yea, ultimatum of God, who has made it all possible. Why doesn't He rain down fire and brimstone on them as He did on Sodom and Gomorrah? That is not God's *usual* way of working. He gives life and grants it an option. He receives no joy from coerced fidelity. His message to His created is, " Choose you. . . whom ye will serve" (Joshua 24:25). He is not interested in serfdom but delights in those who have, like Mary of Luke 10:42, chosen that better dish and will not be dragged away from it. Yes, observation reveals that a living being may choose to live the spiritual or the nonspiritual life, but the Bible pronounces a dying, a judgment, an eternity either in hell or heaven (Hebrews 9:27).

Disobedience by God's special people did not stop with Moses; it continued in their new home, Canaan. This was the result of leaning too much on what they could see and not on faith and trust in God. Israel spent 70 years exiled in Babylon as slaves for that mistake but finally returned to Palestine. They rebuilt the destroyed Temple and continued living the ups and downs of a people dealing with God but also at the same time with sin, carnality, and the devil.

BETWEEN THE TESTAMENTS

Malachi is the thirty-ninth and concluding book in the Old Testament. Four hundred years would elapse before there would be another fresh word from God, which would inaugurate the New Testament era.

This is not to say, however, that there was inactivity in the world. Quite the contrary is true since much was going on.

Persia was ruling the world when the Old Testament was completed but relinquished its jurisdiction to Macedonian control and Hellenistic (Greek) culture under Alexander the Great in 333 B.C. Alexander died in Babylon at age thirty-three and world rule passed to his generals. The new rulers were the Ptolemies of Egypt and those of Syria, who were the Seleucids. The Ptolemies ruled the territory of Palestine first, but in 199 B.C. the Seleucids took over by force. Whereas the Ptolemies had been lenient, their victors were dominating and determined to impose Greek culture upon the Jews. The explosion point was reached under Atiochus IV, surnamed "Epiphanes," which meant "God status." He was determined to destroy the Jews' religion. They were slaughtered and the Temple was desecrated with a pagan image and the sacrificing of swine (an unclean animal to the Jews). Furthermore, the rite of circumcision, Sabbath observance, and the celebration of the feasts of the Jewish calendar were punishable by death. Copies of the scriptures were ordered destroyed.

Jewish Independence

As Antiochus continued his terror, he dispatched an officer to the village of Modin, fifteen miles west of Jerusalem, to force Mattathias, the aged priest, to offer a pagan sacrifice. He refused, and when a timid Jew attempted it, the stalwart of God killed both him and the emissary from King Antiochus. Mattathias and his five sons (John, Simon, Judas, Eleazar, and Jonathan) fled to the hills and began an era of revolt and independence not fully ended until 63 B.C. by Pompey and his Roman legions. Rome ruled the Jews when Jesus was born and the New Testament began. When one has finished studying the Old Testament and greets the New Testament, he is confronted with some strange terms. They are the Septuagint, the synagogue, the Sanhedrin Council (presided over by the high priest), the Sadducees, and the Pharisees.

The Septuagint was a Greek version of the Bible, translated at Alexandria, Egypt, in seventy-two days by seventy-two Jewish interpreters. It was the version in vogue when Jesus walked the earth.

The synagogue is mentioned once in the Old Testament (Psalm 74:8) and sixty-eight times in the New Testament. It was a place in the community for worship, prayer and teaching. Though it probably did not have its beginning during the period between the testaments, it rose to its full height at that time. It was a fully established part of the Jewish community when Jesus arrived.

The Sanhedrin Council embodied seventy-one prominent leaders, learned in Jewish law. The high priest was one of this number. This body tried cases of idolatry and false prophets, but its power to declare the death penalty had been rescinded by the time the group condemned Jesus to death for alleged blasphemy. The charge given to Pontius Pilate, the Roman procurator, was that of treason against Caesar.

The Sadducees (descendants from the priests) were the aristocrats and liberals of Jesus' day. They denounced the doctrine of the resurrection, contending that both soul and body perished together at death. They accepted only the Pentateuch (the Old Testament's first five books) as being authoritative and did not believe angels or spirits existed.

The Apostle Paul used the resurrection to divide the Sanhedrin Council, before which he stood in the city of Jerusalem. The council, composed of both Pharisees and Sadducees, got into a fight when Paul mentioned the subject. It was a means of Paul's escape from them (Acts 23:1-10).

The Pharisees "separated" had their beginning in patriotism and biblical faithfulness, but as with most if not all denominations, they gradually and steadily departed from God's teachings for substitutions of their own (Mark 7:7ff). The very ones who, because of their position, should have recognized and appreciated Jesus vowed to see him dead (John 11:45-54).

A Personal Commentary

In Matthew 21:10-23:39 Jesus is in the Jerusalem Temple for the last time. The time is shortly before His death. How many of us--preachers, deacons, laymen--fit the picture that He paints in this discourse?

- No wedding garment.
- You say and do not.
- You refuse to get under the load.
- You play to men.
- You like to stand out in a crowd.
- You love titles, e.g., "doctor."
- You refuse the servant role.
- You exalt self.
- You make no heavenly converts.
- You pray unqualified prayers.
- Your converts are "children of hell."

11

THE NEW TESTAMENT

The twenty-seven books of the Bible's New Testament are prefaced by the four gospels (good news, glad tidings): Matthew, Mark, Luke and John. The gospels deal essentially with the life of Christ on earth. Reading them is a lofty experience indeed. Following the gospels is the Book of Acts, or The Acts of the Apostles. It has also been referred to as the acts of the Holy Spirit and could well be dubbed the acts of Christ's disciples as they "went every where preaching the word" (Acts 8:4). Nevertheless, the everlasting, universal principle, that action follows being with Jesus, is the poignant point.

The Eternal Unveiling

The epistles (letters), all written by apostles (if Paul wrote the Book of Hebrews), exhort those who are Christians ever to embrace truth and righteousness while shunning error and wickedness. These letters of encouragement and guidance are followed by the last of the sixty-six books in the Bible. The Revelation is its name.

A tremendous and silent mystery is left behind when a person dies. Where is the deceased and in what state is he/she? The eye of flesh does not know. All we mortals know about dying is its fact. It is sure to come to every living being as long as this present world order stands. It visits the great and the small, the wise and the unwise, the renowned and the unknown, the achiever and the failure, the good and the bad. Why has the creator and controller of human life kept what happens to people after death such a secret? Is it not the consensus that nonhuman life ceases with the cessation of earthly life? Yet there is not unanimity of agreement in this matter concerning the future of human life. Many, perhaps the majority, say there is no life beyond the grave for even *Homo sapiens.* This is a nonBiblical, faithless view. The Bible, on the other hand, declares the existence of humanity for all eternity--either in heaven or hell. Throughout His earthly ministry, Jesus often referred to heaven as the final dwelling place for the godly and to hell as the after abode of the godless. One of the most concise descriptions of this afterlife by Jesus is recorded in Luke 16:19-31. How graphicly the account here of the man who went to hell confirms the statement of Hebrews 10:31, "It is a fearful thing to fall into the hands of the living God."

The most complete picture of eternity is that found in the Book of The Revelation, a message of explanation and promise given by God to the Apostle John for the persecuted Christians of Asia Minor. The date is believed to have been A.D. 95 or 96 during the reign of Domitian, the emperor of Rome, A.D. 81-96. Christians were dying in droves for refusing to worship the emperor.

God grants that for which the faithful pray--a confirmation of their choice and trust. He raises the curtain and allows us to look. It's a breathtaking scene! The saints, who were faithful unto death, are shown living and reigning with Christ. The throne of judgment comes into view with all people who ever lived standing before it. Every person is judged according to his/her works. And those whose names have not been written in the book of life are cast into the lake of fire for all eternity. Jesus taught that, at death, the surrendered and forgiven go to heaven; the

13

nonsurrendered (to Christ) and the unforgiven go to hell, where their fate is sealed forevermore. There is no way out. The Bible knows no doctrine such as purgatory. It is a dogma of man, not of God.

THE CHURCH'S BOSS

The boss of the church, locally and institutionally, is the Bible. It, and it alone, is to guide the pastor, the deacons, the congregation, and each individual member. How can we know its true interpretation? By having a born-again heart and a mind of Christian common sense.

As a young and new preacher, who had found God and had been conquered by Him, I began diligently studying the Word of God. I believed then, as I do now, that it would guide me into all truth. If the Bible was for it, so was I. If the Bible was against it, likewise for me. Yes, I am sold on the veracity of the Bible because I cannot imagine our great God creating this fantastic world and designing beings (made in His image) to inhabit and operate it without furnishing them a manual telling how to make it work. I accept and trust the Bible also because of what it claims for itself:

II Timothy 3:16-17

All scripture is given by inspiration of God, and is profitable for doctrine, for reproof, for correction, for instruction in righteousness: That the man [person] of God may be perfect [complete], throughly furnished unto all good works.

14

II Peter 1:20-21

For no prophecy recorded in Scripture [Old Testament] was ever thought up by the prophet himself. It was the Holy Spirit within these godly men who gave them true messages from God (LBT).

These two scriptural passages are only the tip of the iceberg in reference to the Bible's claim that it is the will and Word of God. I believe God has given us His infallible Word in the Bible and that it is to be the final say on all spiritual and moral matters.

The Word of God is honored in Psalm 119, which is the longest chapter (176 verses) in the Bible. I love this chapter and have found great comfort, truth, and joy in it. My two favorite verses are 11 and 105:

Thy word have I hid in mine heart, that I might not sin against thee.

Thy word is a lamp [comfort] unto my feet, and a light [guide] unto my path.

I entered the ministry to follow II Timothy 4:2, which says:

Preach the word; be instant in season, out of season [loyalty always]; reprove, rebuke, exhort with all longsuffering and doctrine.

15

The Judas Goat

The appellation of "Judas," because of Judas Iscariot who betrayed Christ, has lived ever since in infamy. The goats that were used to lead sheep into the slaughterhouse came to be called the Judas goats. I have also found them in the church over a period of fifty years.

It's very sad that people will get in the church as Judas entered the apostolic band, hypocritically. Instead of acting like they love God and the godly, their actions bespeak their love of the devil and sin. They go over the head of the pastor, responsible before God and man in keeping the church in line with God's way and will. They ignore the counsel of dedicated deacons, and in general, work havoc within the church, the body of Christ.

Some of these Judas goats are subtle and cunning as a kitten. Others, by virtue of their secular positions and social standing in the community, enjoy their kingpin rank in the church. But instead of working humbly and harmoniously with the pastor and congregation toward godliness and Word conformity, they judiciously maneuver toward selfish, singular, and secular domination. Then there are those, without class or finesse, who blunderbuss about, stirring a continuous uproar--for one reason or another--in the membership.

Judas Goats I've Known

I met my first Judas goat at ages 11 and 13 in the church my father was pastoring when he died February 4, 1937, from cancer of the gall bladder. This female self-appointed but unchecked usurper told my mother, immediately after we buried my dad, "Mrs. Carraway, you and the children (six) may remain in the parsonage two weeks." She was ousting--in two weeks--a pastor's widow, 300 miles from any of her family (which didn't want to help and never did) and penniless in the clutch of the Great Depression.

However, "Mama No Name" was not finished with forsaking and hurting the Carraways. With nowhere else to turn, Mother put my younger brother and me in an orphanage, operated by the churches of which my dad's last pastorate was a part. This church invited me to spend the allowed two-weeks vacation (if the orphanage resident had anywhere to go) with it in the summer of '38. Mama No Name's son (a deacon) and wife would be my host, and would meet me at the bus station upon my arrival at 9:00 p.m. I, with my battered suitcase and thirty-seven cents in my pocket, appeared on time, but my host didn't. He was nowhere in sight, and had no plans to be. I was thirty miles from my destination. I explained my plight to the desk clerk and asked if I could sleep on one of the wooden benches in the station's waiting room. He graciously consented and I at least had somewhere to spend the night. The next morning, without breakfast, I lugged my luggage out to the gravel road which led to the small community to which I was going. I had stood at the roadside only a few minutes when a 7-Up truck stopped and took me all the way to where I was going. I suppose my guardian angel took care of me that night and morning, for which I am still grateful. After leaving my ride, I walked the short distance across a pasture to where I was to stay while a guest of the church. My host and wife showed no surprise or remorse whatsoever and explained their not meeting

me thusly: Widow Judas Goat had said to them, "I would-
n't bother to meet W. B. at the bus station. Why, with his
personality, he'll have no trouble at all." Only a lost, hell-
bound church member, void of the born-again mystique,
could have practiced such cruelty and managed, from a
conscience standpoint, to live with it. It was also my hostess that pushed me into the church, unsaved, while I was
her guest.

Six Judas goats among my fourteen pastorates stand out in
my memory, but I mention only one more. He was Mr.
Town, Mr. Church, Mr. Everything. Had you asked almost
any member of that community who they'd want to be if
they were not who they were, I believe with all my heart
they would have said this man's name. He towered high
above everyone else in the community, including the
church, in prominence, influence, and authority. He was
nice to people, including his pastor, but there was an exor-
bitant price, unmentioned, of course, attached thereto. All
one had to do to find out the expected recompense was to
challenge anything this individual was doing or wanted to
do. I opposed his leading and participating in the smoking
brigade each Sunday morning on the church property prior
to Sunday School Bible study. The variegated assortment
of pipes, stogies, and cigarettes did not help to create or
maintain the image I was endeavoring to lead the church
to reflect. I believed then, and I believe now, that said
activity was contrary to the Bible and displeasing to Christ,
the Head of the church.

But all I got for my effort was Mr. Church's animosity and
his opposing most of what I tried to lead the church to do--
sometimes it was suggestions I believed he actually favored

but opposed just to get back at me. I knew well that no pastor could buck him (none ever had) and remain, so I got a chance to leave and took it.

Sixteen years later, this man of the god image made a gigantic mistake. The crash came on a Friday and come Monday morning, when the news would be circulated, the fat would be in the fire. He had encouraged and enjoyed a god image, but it was about to be learned and heralded far and wide that he had feet of clay. Rather than face such embarrassment and work through the problem, he committed suicide! His death shook the town, to be sure, but soon thereafter all was back to normal, as it always is. However, no one grieved the death of this dear man more than I.

WHAT SAITH THE SCRIPTURES

The church is the guardian of the Word of God, and as I Timothy 3:15 declares, is the pillar and ground of the truth. This does not mean that we lock up the Word in the church's safe, but the Word of God, containing the words of the Lord, is to be loved, faithfully followed, and proclaimed honestly and fully by the church. What are some pertinent truths preserved in the Bible for us?

- ☻ The importance of "What saith the scripture?" (Romans 4:3, 11:2; Galatians 4:30).

- ☻ Ignorance of the scriptures causes man to err (Mark 12:24).

- ☻ Application of the scriptures makes our hearts burn within us (Luke 24:32).

19

☺ Those eager to know God and truth will diligently search the scripture (Acts 17:11).

☺ The man of God is to be a Bible scholar and strong preacher of the Word (Acts 18:24).

☺ Religious professors, but evil or empty possessors, by-pass the scriptures, changing them to satisfy their own wicked designs (Mark 7:9-13).

☺ The scriptures are vital spiritual and moral nourishment for humankind (Luke 4:4).

☺ Loyalty to the scriptures bespeak godly kinship (Luke 8:21).

☺ Serving the Word is more important than serving physical food (Acts 6:2).

☺ The genuine child of God fills his being with the Word of God (I John 2:14).

☺ Devotion to the Word can cause us to suffer persecution and death (Revelation 1:9, 20:4).

A Stalwart Daughter of God

I will always cherish the memory of Bernice Thacker as a stalwart daughter of God and pillar in her church. She was a devoted wife, mother, and grandmother. Bernice had one pat question when any matter, especially a controversal one, arose in the church, "What does the Bible say?" Amen. The Bible, and it alone, is the boss of the church.

SHAMED BY THE WORLD

Jesus made a profound statement, appropriate for today: "For the children of this world are in their generation wiser than the children of light" (Luke 16:8). What did the unjust steward do that motivated Christ's remarks? He saw, he thought, he did--something God's so-called people are not doing today. And that neglect can only lead to failure and loss. The generation that is currently *kicking the bucket* stands condemned before God.

A Good Pattern to Follow

The unjust steward was a crook and thief unworthy of the trust that his employer accorded him. That's the way swindles are set up and executed, i.e., a good guy (the victim) and a bad person (the con artist). We all deplore the scam man; Jesus does too, but we have to admit that he's clever as a fox. Are we? Or, is what we're doing just plain lethargic and dumb?

What's happened to the spiritual and moral values of this great country? Where did they go? Where is there a man of God today, who will take a biblical stand against garish immorality, e.g., homosexuality (unquestionably condemned in the Bible in Genesis 19:5-11, Deuteronomy 23:17, I Kings 14:24, 15:12, 22:46, II Kings 23:7, Romans 1:26-32); abortion, which is murder; sabbath desecration (divesting of sacred character, diverting from a holy to a profane use); Temple defilement (bringing into the buildings "set-apart" unto God that which pollutes and deviates from the spiritual to the secular); theft of the holy tithe; and other moral issues so emphatically delineated in the

Bible? Where are the John the Baptists who will condemn sin in high places, or the Polycarps who will die rather than back away from Christ and His precepts, or men like Martin Luther who will challenge an impregnable denomination, or the undaunted Bonhoeffers who will crusade against even national contempt for decency and morality?

Yes, the unjust steward of Jesus' story saw, thought, and acted. Shall we of the higher world let one of the lower realm put us to shame? We must not, and we will not!

"Then Moses stood in the gate of the camp, and said, Who is on the Lord's side? let him come unto me. And all the sons of Levi gathered themselves together unto him"
(Exodus 32:26).

ADMITTANCE

How does one of the human species become a child of God and a citizen of heaven? If it's by virtue of the natural birth, Jesus lied and the Bible is abrogated.

Jesus said to a well-thought-of man, "Ye must be born again." The Greek word for again is "anothen," which means "from heaven." So the new birth is not only another birth besides that of the first, it is a spiritual birth from above.

Nicodemus of our story (John 3:1-7) was dumbfounded at Jesus' words. He, a member of the prestigious and powerful Sanhedrin Council at Jerusalem, had no idea there was anything lacking in his life, yet Jesus unhesitatingly told him there was.

The inquirer was aghast at the thought of having to go through the physical birth again. How eerie! However, the Messiah was not speaking of corporeality; he was referring to the spiritual birth. And the heaven-going person has been born twice--once from his earthly mother and once from his heavenly Father.

> That which is born of the flesh is flesh; and that which is born of the Spirit is spirit (John 3:6).

Not only does the new birth fit one for heaven when he or she dies, it equips the recipient for spiritual living while here on earth. In other words, it gives that individual a spiritual heart, which is a prerequisite for serving and walking with God.

> But the natural man receiveth not the things of the Spirit of God: for they are foolishness unto him: neither can he know them, because they are spiritually discerned
> (I Corinthians 2:14).

That's why the unregenerate church member has no appetite for the spiritual aspects of the church. That one is strictly socially-minded and cannot help just tolerating the spiritual while longing for and working toward the secular in the church. The true shepherd of God grieves for such a member and, at the same time, strives to maintain the spiritual nature of the ecclesia. However, sorry to say, his effort usually is to no avail, much to the pastor's consternation and the heartbreak of God.

> And he [Jesus] went into the temple, and began to cast out them that sold therein, and them that bought; saying unto them, It is written, [Isaiah 56:7, Jeremiah 7:11] My house is the house of prayer: but ye have made it a den of thieves (Luke 19:45-46).

As a pastor, called of God to steer the sheep always toward biblical truth, I wore myself out trying to keep Jesus in the church, the devil out of the church, and the true nature of the Body of Christ preserved.

Another by-product of the new birth is a moral heart. Jesus pioneered the way for His followers in this respect as John 8:29 records, "And he that sent me is with me: the Father hath not left me alone; for I do always those things that please him."

Wouldn't it be wonderful if we could do that, i.e., always obey and please God! Yet the child of God, the one with the moral heart, desires to do just that. We insist that we love God with all our heart, mind, soul, and strength--and Jesus said, "If you [really] love Me, you will keep (obey) My commands" (John 14:15, ABT). What's at stake here? Searching the Word of God for what He does/does not want, then endeavoring--day by day--to live in every way according to His will.

HOW TO BE BORN AGAIN

We've thought of what the new birth is; now let us find out how to obtain it. I verily believe that the new birth is one of today's most tainted, most mistaught, and most misunderstood doctrines in the church. If this statement is well grounded, there is cause for horrendous alarm. Jesus said, concerning one who worked against rather than for Him, "Good were it for that man if he had never been born" (Mark 14:21).

Most of the discussions, orally or in print, I've heard concerning how to experience and attain the new birth have upset me no end. Some say, "Believe on the Lord Jesus Christ and thou shalt be saved" (Acts 16:31). That's what Paul and Silas told the Philippian jailer, 'tis true but verse 32 goes on to say, "And they spake unto him the word

25

of the Lord, and to all that were in his house." Simply instructing the quizzical to "believe on the Lord" is not sufficient. The Apostle James, by inspiration, said, "Thou believest that there is one God; thou doest well: the devils also believe, and tremble. But wilt thou know, O vain man, that faith without works [action] is dead?" (James 2:19-20).

What kind of belief does God require in one's receiving the new birth? A complete surrender of oneself to God, trusting Him the rest of one's life with that life--to use as He sees fit. It took me six years, two false professions, two meaningless baptisms, and much agony of soul to discover the key to getting born again! Please allow me to share my salvation experience with you.

My Salvation Experience

Remember: I was born to a preacher and his wife, which indicates that I was in church even before I can remember it. At age ten, I asked my father if I could join the church. His reply was, "Son, joining the church is a very serious thing to do. No one is to do that until he has had a personal experience with God, that is, an assurance that God has accepted him as His child. When that happens, no one will have to tell you. You will know it beyond the shadow of a doubt." He said nothing more, and in a year he was dead.

It wasn't long after my talk with my dad when I raised my hand, by invitation, in a service of our church, indicating my awareness that I needed the new birth. As I now consider my doing that, I doubt the wisdom of the gesture on my part, because I was approached--over and over--by members of the church trying to get me saved. That would have been fine if they had known what they were doing and had their ministering been of any help. It was not. What they said,--"Trust Christ." "Just let go." "Jump into His arms."--made no sense to me, so I continued as I had been. No assurance had come to my heart and no change had come over me.

During my visit with the church in 1938, which I've already reported, revival services were in progress and, of course, I attended. At altar call time of the first service, an elderly deacon came to me and asked if I were a Christian yet. I answered that I was not, which was noised abroad, inviting the wolf pack to move in. Finally my hostess said, "W. B., what's this about you not being a Christian? Why, you're all right. You've been a good boy, sung songs in the church, and even the present evangelist calls you little John the Baptist." She concluded by saying, "You go forward when the invitation is given this morning, make your public profession that you're accepting Christ, then get baptized and you'll be just fine." Not knowing any better, I did exactly as she advised, but it was wasted effort.

By the time I was fourteen, I was singing bass in a junior mixed quartet. Our forte was gospel music with special solo runs for all four parts, which none of us had any trouble accomplishing--to the delight of usually a packed house, I might add. In the summer of '39, the entire quartet was invited to spend our vacation with a church on the Texas Gulf Coast. One Sunday night during the worship service, I became heavily burdened over my empty heart and lost condition. In fact, by the time the service ended, I was sobbing noticeably, attracting the attention of the pastor. He informed me that a group of the members

27

was having a social hour around a freezer of ice cream at his house, which would afford an excellent opportunity for them to pray with me about my need. We met in a semicircle at the parsonage and several prayers were voiced on my behalf. When there was a pause, the pastor's wife said, "Don't you feel better now, W. B.?" At least I had stopped crying, but nothing had happened in my heart. But the dear lady insisted that I was all right now, and the thing for me to do was make my profession the following Sunday and receive (number two) baptism. Again, no peace.

I left the orphanage in the summer of 1942 to live with a foster family in Denison, Texas. It was there I found the Lord. It happened one summer night during revival services at our church. I had entered the building with a heavy heart and plunked down on a bench, all alone in my thoughts as I poured out my heart to God. I did not hear one word the evangelist said or one song that was sung or do I remember who sat by or near me. I silently prayed like I'd never prayed before, "Dear Lord, I'm not your child and I'm going to hell. Please come into my life and make me your own. Place my name on heaven's register, so when the roll is called up yonder, I'll be there." Suddenly, and without warning, a strong impression came over me, "W. B., you keep asking God to do for you; what are you willing to do for Him?" No one had ever suggested such a question to me, neither had I ever thought of it before. (Looking back, I have no doubt that it was either the Holy Spirit or my guardian angel.)

But new or not, I responded immediately in my mind and heart, "That's certainly a fair, logical question and my answer is anything, anywhere, any price, even at the cost of my life." Again, something happened suddenly. I realized I wasn't praying anymore and asked myself why. The thought rebounded that I no longer wanted to pray. Again I asked why. It came into my mind loud and clear: "You got what you want; you have been accepted by God." I sat stunned on that pew and argued with God that it couldn't be true, but the assurance that it was overwhelmed me. I've often said I discovered the truth and ability of the verse in Romans 8:16 long before I even knew it was in the Bible: "The Spirit itself [Himself] beareth witness with our spirit, that we are the children of God."

No, I did not make a public profession that night. I wanted "it" to go away, if it would. I was sick of false professions. I told nobody what had happened for two weeks. Then I shared the good news with my foster mom, and a month after it happened, I made my public profession at a Sunday morning worship service and later received baptism for the first time. The former immersions had been just that-- immersions. Baptism is the immersion in water of a person who has been born-again.

The Key

Eureka! I found it! The key that unlocks God's great salvation is **surrender.** Is that not what Jesus said in Luke 9:23, "If any man will come after me, let him deny [give himself away to me] himself, and take up his cross daily, and follow me"? Jesus saves no one who will not trust Him with his/her very life.

I'm not sure in exactly what vein Judson Van DeVenter (1855-1939) meant it, but he certainly hit the nail on the head when he penned the hymn, "I Surrender All." Like it or not, that's what Jesus Christ requires, even demands, in granting one, by grace, the new birth.

Brotherly Love

Continuing the consideration of the caliber of heart Jesus gives with the new birth (spiritual, moral), let's examine a third characteristic of the redeemed heart. It is that of brotherly and sisterly love. It grieves me to see this beautiful entity dying in our families, churches, communities, state, nation and world.

Fellow feeling is a part of the package Jesus bestows on a receiver of redemption. The capability is there if we'll use it. And the practice of this moral gem is not optional; it is obligatory. Scriptures abound on the subject, but first we start with the preeminent recipient of our adoration:

> Hear, O Israel: The Lord our God is one
> Lord: And thou shalt love the Lord thy God
> with all thine heart, and with all thy soul,
> and with all thy might (Deuteronomy 6:4-5).

Recently, while I was buying office supplies, my clerk and helper was a young, black man. It didn't take long for each of us to sense the other's mystique, which led to animated conversation. My new-found friend excitedly exclaimed, "I really love the Lord!" So did the psalmist, for he said in Psalm 116:1:

> I love the Lord, because he hath heard my
> voice and my supplications.

We are to love God's commands above earthly riches and to learn and believe that those commands are not burdensome; they are a delight and privilege to observe. May we always remember that God's instructions to us were given out of love to us for our good. The scriptures for these two statements are:

> I love thy commandments above gold; yea, above fine gold (Psalm 119:127).

> For this is the love of God, that we keep his commandments: and his commandments are not grievous (I John 5:3).

The second object of our love is to be others, with the same love and care that we have for ourselves. Strong advice? Absolutely, but Jesus is the one who gave it:

> Thou shalt love thy neighbor as thyself (book of Matthew 19:19).

> Therefore all things whatsoever ye would that men should do to you, do ye even so to them: for this is the law and the prophets (Matthew 7:12).

And what a clincher on the subject is this verse:

> A new commandment I give unto you, That ye love one another; as I have loved you, that ye also love one another. By this shall all men know that ye are my disciples, if ye have love one to another (John 13:34-35).

31

Who are the true blue, approved of God? "And he answered . . . My mother and my brethren are these which
hear the word of God, and do it" (Luke 8:21). How may
we know what a preacher or layperson is really on the inside? "By their fruits ye shall know them" (Matthew 7:20).
I am always, in every circumstance, to let "God be true,
but every man [who would contradict Him] a liar" (Romans 3:4). Jesus said that a distinguishing mark of His
child was love for fellow Christians and others" (John
13:35).

What a disappointment it is to see wolves in sheep's clothing. The pretender, the hypocrite is a disgusting sight, yet
that is what one is who professes to be a born-again child
of God but refuses to treat others with respect and gentle-
ness. I entered the ministry fifty years ago to serve God,
to obey His commands, and to treat people like His Word
instructs. I assumed all others who wore the cloth and the
name felt likewise. I was wrong and very gullible.

Deceit

It was in the sixties and I was in my sixth pastorate. One
day a personal letter came to my desk from one of my
denominational leaders, requesting my presence at a seminar that was being conducted under his auspices 300 miles
from me. I knew the man and had shown an interest in the
work he led. The letter drew me like a magnet to that
meeting. I was pleased that my expertise in that realm had
finally been recognized and was about to be utilized. I
wrote Dr. Big Shot that I would attend the meeting and
requested that he reserve my wife and me a room in the
place where I knew he would be staying. I thought it a bit

strange that I had no further word from Dr. Big Shot, but after bringing a lady in to stay with our four children the several days we'd be away, we set sail. Upon arrival, I checked at the desk about the reservations only to learn we had none. A few minutes later I spotted this state Baptist leader with other Big Shots and asked why he did not make the reservation for me. "Huh!" he shot back, "I'm not in charge of reservations."

Then it hit me. That letter to me was not personal; it just looked like it was. It had gone to hundreds of others. Then I was not familiar with the merge feature of computing wherein hundreds and thousands of letters can be sent out with each one appearing like it was typed for just one person. An additional word about this deceiver: he ignored me throughout the three-day conference.

I had been hoodwinked, but what could I do about it? I could recognize this charlatan for what he was and never have anything to do with him again. And that's precisely what I did. Yet my tale isn't told; hold on!

Mr. Big Shot got paid back--with interest. His sin found him out. His family was hit with a terrible malady, taking several lives to date, and he's howling to high heaven. Gloating? No, not at all, but at the same time, I did not write the rules by which we're supposed to live!

Contempt

My church was asked to host a meeting to be led by another representative from the state Baptist headquarters. I'd never met or even heard of him before, so I took what he had to say about "Puzzling Practices among Us" quite seriously. Weeks later, I saw him at one of our area denominational meetings. I spoke; then said, "I, along with you, am concerned about weeds in our Baptist garden and would like to work with you toward some solutions." (I saw nothing at all out of place in such a statement and was not prepared for his reaction.) His red face was filled with contempt as he replied, "I'm not interested in solutions!" Having delivered his bomb, he wheeled around and walked away. To this day, I do not understand his behavior. However, that didn't stop Dr. Mixed Up. Soon he was pastoring a large church in another state, then he got a big one in Texas, and now he heads a liberal organization at a salary of $100,000 a year.

A Summary

A summary of the two episodes just related does not portray the brotherly love taught, yea, demanded, by Jesus. The two perpetrators were out of line with Christlike deportment. If we are to talk the talk, we must walk the walk.

CONCLUSION

Isn't it a priceless possession to have the new birth, obtained through a **surrender** of self to God (the Father, Son, and Holy Spirit since accepting one is embracing all three because They are one and inseparable) and the impartation of this matchless gift by His unspeakable grace?

"And all the people said, Amen, and praised the Lord" (I Chronicles 16:36).

THREE

ASSIGNMENT

God saves us for service. That's what discipleship means. As already shared, God forced me to surrender totally to Him (being anything, going anywhere, paying any price) before He would come into my heart. God not only needs workers in His vineyard, He must have them. His constant call is "Whom shall I send, and who will go for us?" (Isaiah 6:8).

In the antediluvian world, God found only **one man** worth saving. He, like Enoch before him, loved God and walked with Him in close fellowship. His name was Noah. One day God informed His servant that everyone on the earth would be destroyed by a tremendous flood of water except Noah, his wife, and their three sons and their wives. Only eight persons would be left alive upon the face of the earth.

Having revealed His plan and purpose to Noah, God instructed him to build an ark for the saving of his family. The project would take 120 years, during which time Noah pled with the wicked to repent, but in vain. The work would be onerous and the laughingstock of the godless and condemned people of that day, but Noah believed God and did what he was told to do. Now we know he was the wise one and not the demented ignoramus he was accused of being by the foolish and wicked population around him.

A gargantuan duo that made the earth tremble in their day was Elijah and Elisha. Both were riveted to Jehovah in love, obedience, and fearless service (I Kings 17-II Kings 13:21).

Elijah's assignment was to defy the heathenism of his king and queen, Ahab and Jezebel. On the mountain of Carmel, the prophet called down fire from heaven, made monkeys out of the 850 prophets of Baal, proved their religion a hoax, and then slew them. Queen Jezebel, rather than appreciating Elijah's showing all the nation who and where the true God was, swore she would kill him. Her reaction so unnerved the great man of God that he ran out of the country and down to the desert, finally stopping at Mount Horeb after a journey of forty days.

I can empathize with Elijah in this instance, for I've done the same thing. It has taken me fifty years to realize that not all religious people will accept the truth, no matter what God's true representative does or proves. Their evil and calloused hearts will not allow them to say, "I was wrong." It is only those who "have ears to hear" that listen and agree.

But God knew--all the time--where Elijah was and went to him. The Lord's first question was "What are you doing here, Elijah?" That was not where the preacher was supposed to be. Then God demonstrated a vital lesson to Elijah and to us. I have rejoiced in its truth many times. The lesson teaches us what association with God is truly like. It is not like wind or earthquake or fire but the still, small voice of the Spirit. My religion (and my hope) is all wrapped up in the quietness of my heart, and that's ample for me. A current shaving lotion commercial shows a celebrity saying he does not need some fancy cologne to tell him he's a man; he just uses the simple stuff. I say the same thing about my fellowship with God. It's enough for me that "He walks with me, and He talks with me, and He tells me I am His own. And the joy we share as we tarry there, none other has ever known."

After ministering to His man on the mountain, God told Elijah to go back--back to work. He was to anoint a king for Syria, one for Israel, and Elisha as his successor. No matter what others may do, God's man/woman is to go right on faithfully doing the Lord's work.

Other loyals of God in gloriously difficult assignments were Isaiah, Jeremiah, Ezekiel, Daniel, Amos, and Jonah. The prophet of God named Jonah rebelled at God's sending him to Nineveh of Assyria. But the message had to be delivered, Jonah was the one to preach it, and he did it after God got through chastising him.

Why do we resist God's commands and orders? Numerous testimonies have been given by those called of God to preach His precious Word admitting that they fought the call. The "why" is because the work is hard, it demands sacrifice, and it leads to one's earthly unpopularity. Yet for the obedient, who fulfill their commission, there is peace, joy, and fulfillment, despite the rigors of the task.

NEW TESTAMENT CONSIGNEES

Some New Testament faithfuls who wrought for God were John the Baptist, Jesus, and the Apostle Paul, each one dying the death of a martyr. They died for truth, for morality, for God, and for man. As for Jesus, He died for you and me.

When Jesus, the Lamb of God, appeared to the church located at Smyrna in the days of horrible Roman persecution, He admonished the members, "Fear none of those things which thou shalt suffer: behold, the devil shall cast some of you into prison, that ye may be tried; and ye shall have tribulation ten days [a set time and a short time]: be thou faithful unto death, and I will give thee a crown of life" (Revelation 2:10).

Martyrdom

Not all followers of God are required to seal their fidelity with their own blood, but some are. One was Ignatius of Antioch, Syria, who died a martyr's death at Rome during the reign of Emperor Trajan (A.D. 98-117). Another was Pollycarp of Smyrna, who paid for his faithfulness to Christ with his life in A.D. 155 during the persecution of Christians by Roman Emperor Marcus Aurelius. Still another martyr was Dietrich Bonhoeffer, a German, who was hanged by the Nazis (1945) at the age of thirty-nine because he remained true to Christ and openly opposed the evils of Nazism. God's devotee is not eager to die; no one is, but the genuine child of God will forfeit his (dear-to-him) life rather than turn against his Lord by doing what He has forbidden. Nevertheless, God has an assignment for each person--male and female--whom He redeems. That appointment may come at the time of salvation as it did with the Apostle Paul or one's specific and lifetime charge may be revealed later as it was to me. My particular commission came some four years after I received the gracious gift of the new birth.

MY CALL TO THE MINISTRY

I desperately wanted to be saved, but I did not want to be a preacher. It did not appeal to my fleshly nature anymore than it would appeal to anyone else. Yet I had promised God I'd go anywhere, be anything, and do whatever I was asked by Him to do if He personally would come into my life. I had to wait six long years to get what I wanted. He had to wait six months.

I was born December 8, 1925 to a Baptist minister and his wife, the fourth of six children, at Blooming Grove, Texas. My father, H. B. Carraway, was pastor of the First Baptist Church there. Dad was 6'2", slender, nice-looking, and a fireball in and out of the pulpit. He too faced meager financial compensation (as do the majority of ministers when compared with what other trained professionals receive). He was also a victim (so my mother told me) of jealousies and schemes to unseat him and refused to be party to any movement within his pastorate or denomination that he considered not ordered and allowed by his Lord. In fact, I honestly believe, as I have reported many times, that my father cried more than he laughed. That is my way of saying that he was upset most of the time.

Sunday Work Unhoused Us

An illustration of my saying that dad was often in a pickle was the Lord's Day we returned from morning worship to

39

our rented house, only to find the landlady's two grown sons unloading hay in the loft of the barn on the premises. Dad advised them that he and his boys would assist them in their work the following day, but he could not allow them to work on Sunday on the property for which he was responsible. The sons obeyed my father's ultimatum, drove the mules, pulling the haywagon back down to their house, but we moved shortly thereafter.

I am a former pastor of the First Baptist Church in the town of my present residence. One day I stumbled into a member of that church, who began talking about the days of my being his pastor. One of his remarks was "You really took care of the flock (membership), even to the point of sacrifice." Frankly, I didn't know there was any other way. But that was another reason the preaching/pastoring ministry had not appealed to me as a youngster.

A Promise Broken

I've never been able to figure it out, but I finished my high school work with the highest scholastic average of any boy lettering in football. I completed the required work for graduation in December of '43 and was sworn into the U.S. Navy at Dallas in March of '44. After a train ride of several days, I was in boot camp at San Deigo, California. It took only five weeks to get me ready to fight, and a light cruiser, the *U.S.S. Miami*, took a five-day cruise to Pearl Harbor with me and others on it. I've often said that I've been and not been to Hawaii because, though I was there a week, it was spent in the confines of the naval barracks at Barber's Point. I did see a Dole pineapple patch near my quarters and the horrible devastation caused by the

Japanese some three years previously, but that is the extent of my having been to Hawaii. However, only one week after arriving, I boarded a slow freighter and sailed to the Marshall Islands, where the ship to which I had been assigned was anchored.

I boarded the *U.S.S. Cascade*, a destroyer tender, and was informed that I would man a typewriter, along with two other yeomen, in the captain's office. I'll always remember that sojourn because the captain would not sign anything that had a mistake or correction on it. As you've probably guessed, the three of us did a lot of retyping. I was fortunate to have learned the touch typing system in Denison High School under a kind and patient teacher, Ms. Bertha Knaur, later Mrs. E. G. Johnson. It afforded me good duty in the Navy, and has aided me in many ways since. No sooner had I landed in my permanent home, for seventeen months, when another yeoman (from Hillsboro, Texas), Wayne Dandridge, came agrinning and shaking my hand. We have remained friends for almost fifty-two years and correspond regularly now.

Good Duty

Life aboard the *Cascade* was very comfortable and good, considering the alternative, which was transferring to a different ship that was constantly seeing firing-line duty. No, thanks! Our workday was eight hours, more or less. We had good chow, usually comfortable places to sleep, a movie on the top deck each evening after supper, and varied types of entertainment from time to time. I participated in two boxing smokers (as our boxing programs were called), and several celebrities came aboard, among whom

41

were Eddie Peabody, the banjo king; Jackie Cooper, the movie star; Claude Thornhill, band leader; and others. Richard Ney, who was then married to Greer Garson, was aboard our ship often, as we serviced the destroyer on which he served. We also had regular religious services and, best of all, stayed at a safe distance, back in various harbors, from the battle zone.

Soon after my arrival, we were assigned a new chaplain, who was a Southern Baptist with impressive credentials. He was a graduate of Baylor University, Waco, Texas, and Southern Baptist Seminary, Louisville, Kentucky. I even served as his yeoman at one time, never noticing any behavior that was out of line. However, he was a homosexual and was caught in the act at his first postwar pastorate. He left the ministry, worked in some type of business, and then died rather quietly and mysteriously. We had a ship's quartet, in which I sang bass and we often sang at services aboard our ship. John Ward, another Southern Baptist and now retired from the SBC Annuity Board, was our lead singer. I hesitate to admit it, but I remember only one thing our chaplain said. It was one of his illustrations:

> "Old man," said the defiant youth, "I'd give the world to have what you've got." The elderly gentleman replied, "Young man, that's exactly what it cost me."

Back in the USA

When the war ended for us in August of 1945, we moved from Okinawa to Wakayama, Japan; then I received orders to board a transport ship to San Pedro, California where

42

awaited a week of freedom from responsibility, relaxation, and visiting some of the interesting places in Los Angeles. Then I climbed aboard a train headed for Dallas and a thirty-day leave. The first shore duty of my naval career would be coming up after that in New Orleans, Louisiana, to which I had never been. Everything now was coming up roses.

My days at home in Waxahachie, Garland, and Denison were happy ones, but at the end of my leave, a strange thing happened. My pastor asked me to speak at the Wednesday night service, something I had not asked for or even remotely expected. I chose a Psalm, read it, tried to explain and apply it the best I could, then sat down. Much to my chagrin, C. B. Stanley, president of the Texas Baptist Children's Home in Waxahachie, rose to his feet in that Farley Street Baptist Church to say, "We have just heard one who will preach the gospel as his father did." He and my late dad had been college classmates and good friends through the years. Again I was shocked, almost vexed. Others in the service stood to sanction his remarks. I did not want to hear what I was hearing because, as I've said before, I did not want to be a preacher. I had other ideas for my life.

The next morning I dropped by Pastor L. H. Raney's office to say a final goodbye on my way to the bus station and the trip to New Orleans. We talked briefly and then he said, "W. B., what is your reaction to the people saying last night that you will be a preacher?" My reply was instantaneous, "Brother Raney, if God wants me to preach, He'll have to tell *me*, not someone else." We left it at that and I departed.

The bus ride to New Orleans (from early morning to midnight) was pleasant because I sat by a young lady from Mississippi, who looked very much like a girl I had dated in high school. Her look-alike and I had a most pleasant journey that day and night.

My World Falls Apart

I did a very wrong and foolish thing that day of my heading for the festive city on the mighty Mississippi during the first shore duty of my naval career. I had a carnal good time on my mind, not prayerfully seeking the best way to honor and serve my Lord. That is to say that I had broken my promise (of salvation night) to God. Shame on me!

Upon arrival in New Orleans, I reported to the Naval Air Station on Lake Pontchartrain, where I would join a long line of yeomen assigned to typewriters in a huge hangar, mustering out sailors for the next six months. The war was over and most of us were going home to civilian life.

Completely without warning, I became deeply depressed, even disoriented to an extent. While viewing an on-base movie one evening, for instance, something inside my body literally snapped. My problem became severe enough that I visited an on-the-base physician. All at once I had lost my zest for living. I tried to fight it, guided by the mental plan I had mapped out, but to no avail. Even the French Quarter, with all its glitter, did not assuage the emptiness of my heart nor did the St. Charles Theater, where the stars of stage and screen appeared. Neither the pretty civilian girls who also worked in the hangar at Pontchartrain nor the Sugar Bowl football game New Year's Day of

1946 did anything to slow down my racing heart. Nothing--
absolutely nothing--looked good, tasted good, or felt good.
That's a pitiful state in which to find oneself. That was not
the way I had planned it.

Typing up discharge forms by rote, I floundered and
searched for an answer to my unexpected dilemma. Then
one day, I received a simple postcard from C. D. Arnold,
pastor of a small church on Genois Street, east of Canal
Street, the main drag in New Orleans. He had gotten my
name from the preacher, who, by the way, was preaching
(to deaf ears) the night I came to know God in a personal
and salvation way. He had received my name from my
sister, a member of his church in Corsicana, Texas. The
card from Pastor Arnold cordially invited me to church.

A Lot of Church, and Peace At Last

Regular church attendance and fellowship with a kind
pastor and wife began thawing me out from my perplexity.
I was back in the kind of atmosphere God expected of me,
and I was getting the spiritual/moral nourishment so vital
to Christian peacefulness and growth.

On the night of May 1, 1946, I left the Algiers Naval Station, to which I had been transferred, rode the ferry across
the Mississippi River and upon hitting the north end of
Canal Street, I momentarily pondered how I would spend
this night's liberty. "Liberty" to a sailor is the privilege of
leaving the base for whatever he wants to do--so long as
he behaves himself and stays out of trouble. As I stood on
North Canal Street considering my options for enjoying the
six hours that had been handed to me, I remembered that

45

the church I had been attending had a six o'clock service, and I was drawn in that direction. Upon leaving that service, with plenty of evening left, I searched for another way to spend it, or at least part of it. Of all the happenings in the city that came to mind, the revival service at the First Baptist Church on St. Charles Street was the most appealing. So, again the same evening, to church I went. The pastor was J. D. Grey, and Byron Clifford, a new sensation, was the evangelist. I enjoyed the service, but remember nothing spectacular about it. (Clifford would later get hooked on dope and booze, becoming a vagabond and dying a tragic death.) I returned to my naval barracks, gathered my stationery and pen from my locker, and climbed the stairs to the writing room. By the time I had written several letters and was ready to answer one from Mother, who lived in Waxahachie, it was past midnight, and the room had emptied--except for me.

Mother was aware of my spiritual struggle and had been praying for me. To demonstrate the depth of her concern, she had even enlisted her pastor (and mine) as a prayer partner. When I got down to the heart of my epistle to her, I wrote that I was ready to surrender fully again my life, my will, my all to God. I proceeded to list ways I would serve Him vocationally, but scratched each one out after writing it. I kept pushing the preaching idea away as it, of course, kept coming to mind. Finally, I boldly scrawled that God was truly calling me to the ministry, as we termed it, and I was complying! I flatly refused to erase that sentence, whereupon peace and stability filled my being. I went downstairs to my bunk and slept soundly. **The date was May 2, 1946, and the time was 2:00 a.m.** When Mother received my letter, she happily spread the word to those

46

who would be interested. Only a short time of navy life remained for me, which was spent in living for Christ and getting ready to keep my promise and prepare for the ministry. Truly, they were happy and exciting days!

Ordained

In June of 1946, I had the distinct privilege of mustering myself out of the U.S. Navy after a tenure of some twenty-six months. After celebrating my discharge with that ex-girl friend of high school days I mentioned earlier, *and her Air Force husband*, I entrained to Dallas.

Since I was widely known among the churches of the Baptist Missionary Association of Texas, due to having been in many of them as the bass singer in the Junior Quartet of the Texas Baptist Orphanage, as it was then called, I had enough preaching invitations to fill the summer. In August I was called to my first church at Concord, Texas near Mount Enterprise. It was a half-time church, having services every other Sunday. I also bought my first car--a 1941 black, Chevrolet Business Coupe.

The Concord church called for my ordination, and so it took place at the Farley Street Baptist Church, Waxahachie, Texas on September 6, 1946. My ordaining council consisted of some twenty preachers and two deacons. Hollace Combs, who would become my father-in-law the following February, sang, accompanied at the piano by his beautiful and talented daughter, June who would soon become my wife and later the mother of my four children. John Ward, my navy buddy and lead singer in the *Cascade* quartet, also sang. A full house witnessed the service.

47

Soon thereafter, the First Baptist Church, Beckville, Texas, called me as pastor to fill the other two Sundays of each month. So I was full up with church work as well as being a freshman at Jacksonville College, Jacksonville, Texas, a school my father had attended beginning in 1915.

My Most Prized Possessions

I, like many of our day, am blessed with many earthly treasures, including a well-equipped office with plaques, pictures, diplomas, etc., covering the walls, but my two most cherished material properties hang behind my desk, one on top of the other. First is the ordination certificate of my father, dated July 28, 1915, by the McClung Baptist Church of Kerens, Texas, granting the request of the Oak Grove and Montfort Baptist churches that their pastor, H. B. Carraway, be ordained. W. H. Perry was moderator, Arnon Carraway, Dad's brother, was clerk, and the remaining ordination council members were the Reverend T. E. Lucus and deacons G. W. Simmons, H. B. Jones, and W. L. McDavis.

My ordination certificate, already described, hangs immediately under that of my father. I also have the Bible he was using at the time of his death. These two items are the sum total of my inheritance from Dad's estate, but I have always considered myself richly endowed--and do to this day.

FOUR

CONFIRMATION
(MY BURNING BUSH)

Moses saw a miracle before his very eyes. So did I. For the lawgiver, it was a bramble bush afire somewhere on the mountain of Sinai. For me it was a demonstration of God in a small East Texas church. The burning, but unconsumed, bush stopped Moses in his tracks, drawing his attention to the wonder before him. The burning bush of my experience left me in awe and convinced that God was alive, attentive, cooperative (with His chosen leader), and able to manipulate people like puppets on a string if He so chooses.

Two Churches

I began 1947 pastoring two half-time churches which were located at Beckville and in the community of Concord, five miles east of Mount Enterprise, Texas. Both churches voted in January to go full-time, both calling me as pastor. Therefore, a big decision faced a twenty-one year-old preacher, who had been pastoring only five months.

The First Baptist Church of Beckville was much the better church materially. It had a larger community, the church was positioned right in the middle of the small town, the facilities were nicer, and it paid a higher pastor's salary than that of Concord. I took very seriously the choice

49

that was mine to make. After all, I was in this business (the greatest business in the world, in my opinion) because of a deep, personal, and abiding conviction that God had given me the ministry as His lifelong assignment for me. I sincerely wanted my choice to be His as to where I would serve Him at that time.

Considering that, I talked it over with Him, saying I did not know which congregation's call to accept, but I did know that I couldn't accept both. Therefore, since I was human, as well as spiritual, I would accept the one more attractive to the human eye because that would be the more sensible decision to make from the human stand-point. Is that not the way it's done in the secular world? Nevertheless, I told the Lord that I would not be adamant about it and requested a sign as He gave Gideon twice recorded in the book of Judges 6:1-40. Gideon named wet fleece, dry ground/dry fleece, wet ground as his sign while my sign was to be at least one addition to the church at Concord the following Sunday. Concord was expecting my answer, yea or nay, that Sabbath.

So I made God a proposition: I would stay at Concord, forfeiting Beckville, if that be His will, but only if He made His choice for me unmistakably plain. I stipulated, "If I am to remain at Concord, give us at least one addition to the church Sunday." I felt rather safe since there had been no additions the five months of my tenure and no prospects of any right then as far as I knew.

Sunday came, we had Sunday School, and then I conducted the morning worship service. Having delivered the sermon, I gave the invitation for additions to the church. Stanzas one and two were sung without a stir. I was feeling good. We began the third and final stanza, which I considered just a matter of form, and then I would tender my resignation as Concord's pastor. Abruptly, I heard a stirring from the left side of that white frame auditorium. Then I saw a lady, I would say in her early sixties, pop out into the aisle and head toward me. I extended my hand as she said, "Pastor, I don't know what I'm doing up here. My name is Lena Beasley from Mississippi (?), and I'm on my way to California to visit my son. I stopped off last night to visit my sister, Mrs. Butler, who lives in this community, before continuing my journey. I wanted to attend church this morning but had no idea of asking for membership. Suddenly, I was compelled to come forward."

We accepted Mrs. Beasley on promise of a letter from her out-of-state Baptist church, and I announced my acceptance of the Concord church without further explanation. What had just happened was strictly between God and me. Mrs. Beasley never completed that particular journey. She remained with her sister awhile, then married a widower by the name of Johns of the community and died there.

The Happening Reviewed

Surely, it's no surprise to hear me say that such an occurrence burned an abiding reverential respect (even fear) in me for God. Is God actually aware of what each of us on earth is doing? Honestly now, does He hear and answer prayer? Come on, get real! Would God pay any attention to a poor, orphaned boy, pastor of a church in an obscure place (according to worldly evaluation)? Could this One of omniscience (if such a being even exists) have

51

any interest whatsoever in what this church did or did not do? Would One as great as God would have to be take time out from His busy and more important schedule to give a sign from Heaven to an unknown preacher in a small, country church?

Needless to say, this divine act and experience got my attention! I've gone back to it many times in my mind, trembling each time it's recalled. If there were any doubt in my mind about God knowing, seeing, caring, it was all erased in that event of January, 1947. This was God's confirmation to me of His awareness of our every move and of His having a design for each of His own. The experience at Concord, near the beginning of my preaching ministry for God, taught me something else too. It was that I would always be more attracted to the place of dire need than to one where all the hard work was completed.

The Apostle Paul said in Romans 15:20-21 that he did not care to build upon another's foundation but preferred to plow new ground for Christ. Paul articulated my sentiments precisely. Since I like to work (actually enjoy it), I have always been attracted, in Christ's service, where there is work to be done. It is a tremendous fulfillment to see the work of the church started, or strengthened in a locality, a part of which I enjoy being. Why? Simply answered: That's where my heart is.

Another reason the place of need is appealing is because God pays dividends only for work done. No work for Christ, no wages paid by Christ! Since I became a preacher fifty years ago I have been interested primarily in two things: having the strong peace of Christ, which is beyond human comprehension, in my heart, and the privilege of accumulating heavenly and eternal dividends. Only he who works gets paid. Applicable scriptures regarding rewards are Matthew 10:41-42, I Corinthians 3:8 and 9:7, the book of Colossians 2:18, II John 8, and Revelation 22:12. Biblical verses pertaining to our receiving a crown are found in II Timothy 4:8, James 1:12, I Peter 5:4, and Revelation 2:10 and 3:11.

AFTER CONCORD

I married Belva June Combs of Jacksonville, Texas, on February 1, 1947; graduated from junior college in May, 1948; moved to Sherman, Texas, and Austin College; and welcomed our first child, the late Donald Bryan Carraway, October 24, 1948. Planning to enroll at Baylor University, Waco, Texas, for the completion of my college work, I changed my mind at the last moment, due to the persuasion of a preacher friend. I made the Sherman move to become missions director for the Grayson County Baptist Association (BMA). I was editor of the Kangaroo, school newspaper at Austin College, was a member of the student council, and was on the debate team. My mission work of one year saw a new BMA church begun in Sherman.

The BMA Splinter

An unfortunate thing happened back in Jacksonville before my wife and I left. Her father, a Jacksonville College faculty member and music minister at the First Baptist Church, became the center of controversy over some of his convictions and teachings. Subsequently, he was terminated by both institutions. This, and other problems, precipitated a splinter (the departure was not large enough legitimately to be labeled a split) in the denomination. It also placed me in an unenviable position. Because of the animosity toward my wife's father in the BMA (of that time), it would have made my working any longer therein very difficult--on my part as well as that of others. My alternative was not to my liking. I refer to the group with which I suddenly found myself associated. Consequently, I had a problem, but really known only to the Lord and me. It was one that He solved.

I BECOME A SOUTHERN BAPTIST

In August of 1949, ready for my senior college year, I became a Southern Baptist by accepting the pastorate of the First Baptist Church of Nash, Texas, five miles west of Texarkana, Texas, on Highway 82. My opportunity there was due to no effort at all on my part.

My wife's aunt, who lived in nearby Hooks, submitted my name to the Nash Pulpit Search Committee. I was contacted, I spent a Sunday with the church and the congregation wanted to select me as its pastor, but when actually put on the spot, I found myself getting cold feet. I'm sure that feeling is understandable. I had heard the SBC demeaned all my life (I was now twenty-four), and I knew I would be buried by the BMA brethren if I "deserted." For the record, my fears were corroborated through the ensuing years with malicious words and unbrotherly treatment. This was extremely unfair because I entered my new affiliation just as determined to stay true to God and the Word as I had ever been. I told the Nash church just that. Due to my dubiousness toward accepting the church's call, we agreed on a series of services, lasting a week. Then a decision concerning our becoming aligned as pastor and people would be made. My preaching was eagerly and appreciatively accepted with our having a good week. A unanimous call which I accepted was extended. After filling some already made commitments, my wife, our one-year-old son, and I moved into the neat, two-bedroom, white, frame parsonage beside the church building fronting Highway 82. I had been in the ministry three years, and this was our first parsonage. We were not only grateful, but excited.

A Humorous Incident

One day, as I was mowing the front yard of the parsonage with a push mower (1950, remember), a car drove up on the adjacent churchyard and a man disembarked. I spoke and he said, "Son, I'm looking for the pastor of this church." I replied, "Friend, you're looking at him!"

Roger Baxter, living at New Boston, Texas, was director of the association of churches to which the Nash church belonged. After my installation as pastor, he was talking with one of the members, T. Ray Henderson, about their calling a BMA preacher as pastor. "Will he support our cooperative work?" the director asked. Henderson replied, "He said all of it that was worthy, biblical, and God-honoring," to which Baxter countered, "It all is!" Yet when I left the church two years later, he said to my successor, "You won't have any trouble here. Carraway tied these people to the church, not to himself." I not only appreciated those gracious words but felt I had gained Brother Baxter's commendation and friendship, which were reward enough. I had gotten off to a good start in my first SBC church.

Two other rewarding things happened during my family's days at Nash. In May, 1950, I graduated number fourteen in a class of 140 from Henderson State University, located in Arkadelphia, Arkansas, and on September 14, our family increased to four, with the birth of our second son, Ronald Marvin Carraway.

The Nash experience of two years was a good one. The people were very kind to us and a pleasure to work with. The church grew in membership, and plans for a much-needed auditorium were adopted. Ten thousand dollars was in the building fund when we moved from the church and it wasn't too long until my family and I were invited back for the dedication of the new building. I remember the day well because of the gracious, public words of one of the guests of the day, J. Howard Williams, president of the Southwestern Baptist Seminary, Ft. Worth, where I was a student. Those words were, "How in the world did a fellow like W. B. Carraway ever get such a beautiful wife!" President Williams was a wonderful man.

VIOLATION

God's Word--spoken or written--is to be conscientiously and obediently observed. The true child of God will do just that, counting it a privilege and joy. He who merely pretends spirituality will not, for he cannot. "So then they that are in the flesh cannot please God" (Romans 8:8). The same Spirit who entered the child of God's heart at conversion will enable God's own to obey His word--that is, if that one will dig down deeply (beneath his fleshly nature) for the potential strength that's available for the sincere-- and separated--one.

SCRIPTURES ON OBEYING GOD

O that there were such an heart in them, [God says of His people] that they would fear me, and keep all my commandments always, that it might be well with them, and with their children for ever" (Deuteronomy 5:29).

David's prayer in the twilight of his life for Solomon, his son:

Give unto Solomon my son a perfect heart, to keep thy commandments, thy testimonies, and thy statutes (I Chronicles 29:19).

> Let us hear the conclusion of the whole matter: [concerning earthly life] Fear God, and keep his commandments: for this is the whole duty of man" (Ecclesiastes 12:13).

> If you [really] love Me you will keep (obey) My commands" (John 14:15, ABT).

> Ye are my friends, if ye do whatsoever I command you (John 15:14).

GOD'S MOVE AGAINST DISOBEDIENCE

God makes no exceptions in expecting biblical conformity from His followers. This statement is spectacularly sanctioned by what God threatened to do to one of His greatest leaders of all times. The account is recorded in Exodus 4:24-26.

Moses, who had already been through much because he was God's man, was on his way from Midian (where he had been for forty years) to Egypt for the purpose of leading the Israelites to the Promised Land. En route, God threatened to kill him! Why? For the black sin of disobedience.

The Mosaic entourage stopped for the night at "a stopping place" (wherever that may have been), and God struck Moses, the great one, with a nigh-unto-death illness. **It was a deliberate move of God, not just a happenstance.** Moses got careless. He neglected to do to his son what God had commanded be done to all male Israelites--he had not circumcised him. Moses error could have been the

58

results of an earlier one, i.e., being unequally yoked with Zipporah, a Midianite, who was his wife and mother of his two sons, Gershom and Eliezer. Zipporah, realizing both what the problem was and that her husband, Moses, was too ill to perform the operation, took a flint knife and accomplished the required rite herself. Moses was relieved of his illness and continued the journey after sending his wife and sons back to Midian.

God's drastic act here clearly shows that none is exempt from obeying Him, i.e., no one is above the law of God. God expects His principles, teachings, and commands to be quickly and completely carried out. All who profess to be God's child and servant are diligently to live the Word, teach the Word, and lead others to honor the Word by their obedience to it.

GODLY COMMANDS IGNORED BY MANY

I cringe when I see any of *us* not adhering to God's requirements. Some of the most flagrant violations of His law are herein listed:

Living One's Life for Self

The Apostle Paul, in his sermon on Mars' Hill in Athens, Greece, declared that God "now commandeth all men every where to repent: because he hath appointed a day, in the which he will judge the world in righteousness by that man whom he hath ordained" (Acts 17:30-31). That means that all human life is to give itself--voluntarily and without reservation--to the creator and controller of this mysterious and magnificent universe, desiring His unerring direction

of that life. The complying will be claimed by God, blessed, and accorded a place with the Godhead, angels, and
redeemed of the ages for all eternity in heaven. The non-
submissive will be denied those provisions for the redeemed, receiving instead that reserved for the damned.
Jesus' words make the subject even clearer:

> Let your light so shine before men, that they
> may see your good works, and glorify your
> Father which is in heaven" (Matthew 5:16).

> Jesus taught (Matthew 6:19-21) to be careful
> about what we consider here our treasure
> because, where one's treasure is, there will
> his heart be also.

> Jesus also, in this great Sermon on the
> Mount, decreed it impossible to play both
> sides [heaven and the world, another way of
> saying, God and Satan] when He declared,
> Ye cannot serve God and mammon (money,
> earthly possessions)" (Matthew 6:24).

I was decrying Sunday athletics one evening with some
men of the church on the church grounds of a pastorate
when a leader of the church's Royal Ambassador program
for boys retorted, "You're just jealous because it isn't you
out there enjoying what he is enjoying." His words--twenty-
nine years ago--still ring in my ears as the honest, impul-
sive reaction of a worldly church member, bereft of the
Spirit within, who was on his way to hell! His words, yea,
his condition grieved me to the depths of my soul. If that
man had possessed a born-again attitude, he would have

known that I had no desire to violate the holy Sabbath by disregarding the God-established rules designed for its observance. I want, deep down in my heart, to do things God's way, not mine.

As we continue thought on breaking godly commands by living one's life to suit not God, but oneself, note the words in Mark 8:34-36:

> And when he had called the people unto him with his disciples also, he said unto them, Whosoever will come after me, let him deny himself, and take up his cross, and follow me. *For whosoever will save his life shall lose it;* but whosoever shall lose his life for my sake and the gospel's, the same shall save it. *For what shall it profit a man, if he shall gain the whole world, and lose his own soul?*

In this section, we're discussing the individual, of course, who lives life for self and strictly the way he chooses, with no thought of God, others, or eternity. **Jesus called such a one a fool!** Listen:

> The fool hath said in his heart, There is no God" (Psalm 14:1).

There are two ways, possibly, of interpreting this passage:

The fool here is an atheist, i.e., no God exists.

The fool referred to is saying, "Even though there may be a God, I say no God for me. I will run my own life."

After relating the story of the "rich fool" who planned his retirement without any thought of God in it, Jesus said:

> Thou fool, this night thy soul shall be required of thee: then whose shall those things be, which thou hast provided? So is he [a fool] that layeth up treasure for himself, and is not rich toward God (Luke 12:20-21).

Fear Hell

Should we humans fear hell? Definitely! Why? Because of what the scriptures say:

> The wicked shall be turned into hell, and all the nations that forget God (Psalm 9:17).

> And fear not them which kill the body, [said Jesus] but are not able to kill the soul: but rather fear him which is able to destroy both soul and body in hell (Matthew 10:28).

Reverencing the Sabbath

One of the vilest sins in the catalog is that of Sabbath desecration. What does the perversion (changing its purpose) of the Lord's Day proclaim? It bespeaks the lack of a love and respect for God. Remember: If we love Him, we keep His commandments. The key to respecting the Sabbath (which is one day out of seven kept holy) is God's love in one's heart. God's child will not spend the Sabbath any way but by worshipping and resting. A Presbyterian minister who forfeited the opportunity to play professional football said that one of the reasons for his decision was because he did not want to play football on Sunday. So he chose the ministry instead. What is the basis for a holy Sabbath, which many Christians observe on Sunday? The scriptures! Hear portions of Exodus 20:8-11:

> Remember the sabbath day, to keep it holy. Six days shalt thou labour, and do all thy work: But the seventh day is the sabbath of the Lord thy God: in it thou shalt not do any work. . . For in six days the Lord made heaven and earth, the sea, and all that in them is, and rested the seventh day: wherefore the Lord blessed the sabbath day, and hallowed it.

Sunday, our Sabbath, is not a day for vocational and/or personal work unless there is no reasonable way of getting around it. Sunday isn't for selling (Nehemiah 13:15) or buying (Nehemiah 13:15-18); neither is it a date to be polluted (Isaiah 56:2,6) or a period for personal pleasure (Isaiah 58:13). It is a day of delight (Isaiah 58:13); it is not one to be dreaded, endured, and hated (Amos 8:5).

How should we of these last years of the 20th century observe the Sabbath? It should be an occasion for public worship, an opportunity for rest, a day of refraining from secular work (if at all possible), and twelve hours in which we give even extra attention to reflecting on God. Furthermore, it is not a day for recreation or home chores or going out to eat. (Yuk! I'll be skinned for this, but eating out on the Sabbath is disobeying the stipulation of not buying or selling.) If we want to do what God asked, we

63

will treat His Sabbath request just like we deal with the other nine of the Ten Commandments, which are recorded in Exodus 20:1-17 and Deuteronomy 5:6-21.

God's Holy Tenth

Is money necessary in carrying on the work of the Lord's church in this, His world? Yes. Did He suggest a plan? He did more than that; He passed a law--the law of the tithe. Is that all? No, He also allowed/allows offerings above the tithe, if given from a willing heart (Exodus 35:5). But let us remember that we pay the tithe; we give the offering.

Why do we **pay** (not give) the tithe? Because it is not ours; therefore, we cannot give it. It is money that belongs to God, and if we keep it, God said we have broken the commandment: "Thou shalt not steal." We read Leviticus 27:30:

> And all the tithe of the land, whether of the
> seed of the land, or of the fruit of the tree,
> is the Lord's: it is holy unto the Lord.

In this verse, we have the tithe as a law of God. But in Malachi God reminds us of that law again, commanding us to honor it and promising us a bountiful blessing if we do. Enjoy with me Malachi 3:8-10:

> Will a man rob God? Yet ye have robbed
> me. But ye say, Wherein have we robbed
> thee? In tithes and offerings. Ye are cursed
> with a curse: for ye have robbed me, even
> this whole nation. Bring ye all the tithes into

the storehouse, that there may be meat in
mine house, and prove me now herewith,
saith the Lord of hosts, if I will not open you
the windows of heaven, and pour you out a
blessing, that there shall not be room enough
to receive it.

God's Word (Hebrews 12:6-11) informs us that He chastens every one of His children. Strange as it may seem at first, it is not only true but gracious, in that it reveals His love and care. What about His chastising those who aren't His own? He doesn't; they're not His. They belong to another (the devil). God is not concerned that they be brought to righteous living; He is interested in their repentance, first. Unfair? Not at all. The unredeemed have, according to holy writ, all eternity to pay and suffer for their hostility toward a loving God.

All of God's children tithe--either willingly or by coercion. If it is voluntary, there is a blessing. If God must collect it, there is a curse. These two statements are only a reiteration of Malachi 3:8-10. I not only say this from the Word; I say it from experience! A part of my rebellion, described later, was not tithing. When God punished me, He collected the same amount ($30,000) that I had stolen from Him.

By the way, did Jesus teach tithing? Yes. Where? Luke 18:12, Matthew 23:23, and through the writer of Hebrews 7:5-9.

I must say one final word on this subject: I marvel at church members, claiming to be blood-bought, born-again, heaven-going children of God, who invalidate tithing for themselves and try to prevent others from doing it. They are dead wrong. Not only that, but they're suspect. Are they really saved? Where is that redeemed, supple, obedient, liberal heart? That's the kind God gives with the new birth.

THE TRUE IMAGE OF THE CHURCH

The biblical description of the church (a body of God's born-again children) does not match up with churchdom of the last half of the 20th century. The departure began to make itself known to those with spiritual perception in the sixties. That is to say that the secular, worldly, social, spiritless element that had always been present in a local congregation, but held in check, began forging to the forefront by getting more and more defectors and sympathizers. That movement, aided by a lethargic and spineless membership, has now eclipsed the real picture of our Lord's body, the church. Alarming news, indeed.

What brought about this distorted view of the heavenly institution? Neglect of the Word of God. People stopped reading the Bible and started watching one another. What they saw others doing, and not doing, became the standard. What God said through His Word and His mouthpiece, the preacher, began to be ignored, even fought if need be. The church was becoming what it now is--a worldly entity from which the Spirit of God has departed. R. G. Lee, the late pastor of Bellview Baptist Church, Memphis, Tennessee, told us repeatedly at conventions in the dear days beyond recall that some of the churches in our land were so cold spiritually, one could skate down the aisles on Sunday morning. Sadder than that is the fact that many of today's

66

parishioners are so "far out of it," they don't even know that Christ Jesus isn't there anymore. Oh yes, the machinery continues to run with goals set, meetings (many) held, projects planned and even completed, abundant hoopla multitudinous activities, but all of which is unoiled by the Spirit and repugnant and repellent to the discerning, spirit-filled child of God.

How did this apostasy spread throughout a particular denomination? By various and politicking individuals moving into positions of denominational leadership, who fashioned and promoted the only kind of program of which they were capable--a shallow and secular one. A devoted pastor finds himself in somewhat of a predicament, i.e., trying adequately to shepherd his flock and, at the same time, pleasing denominational leaders.

As a pastor for forty-two years in the largest Protestant denomination in the world, I participated in many meetings and endeavors because I was expected to, but I knew they were essentially a waste of time and money. I praised God the day I was released from that empty wastefulness and could spend more time in Bible study, prayer, and meaningful Christian service.

Yes, the true image of the church, currently, has been besmirched. Distinguishing marks have been adopted that are not compatible with the teachings of Christ, who instituted the church and is its Head. The Master told us that we were all brethren, abolishing the Big Dog, Little Dog classification but that fact has been ignored and is practiced right and left. Today's clergy need to restudy, prayerfully and carefully Matthew 23:1-12.

The Size Heresy

Since actions speak louder than words, it doesn't take long to realize that all churches in the denomination are not equal. The larger ones rule the roost. They have more members, they put more money into the denominational coffer, and their pastors dominate the convention platforms and committees. The smaller churches and their pastors are to be seen, they are to cooperate in every way, but they are not to be heard. Yet all the time, the "big boys" are shouting, if they can be heard above the unchecked corridor noise, "Equality!" Just rhetoric.

At first I, as a new member in my denomination, went along with the trend that all these brothers of the bigger churches were something extra special and could even charm the devil. But the longer I heard them, as compared with the high hours I was spending in solitude with my Bible, concordance, Bible dictionary, commentaries, and godly men of the past who had written their comments on the scriptures, the less enamored I became. It finally dawned on me that what they were saying and stressing was quite mediocre.

I didn't enter the ministry to play; I answered God's call to preach, pray, and progress.

It took awhile for me to see through the folly of Mr. Fly-by-Night, but by listening, thinking, and investigating, I soon did. I quickly learned two things about denominational leadership, the ones who could put you on programs and platforms. They threw out reverse, the hoe, and the question mark (the negative). If one was making a show

68

in his pastorate, without being checked as to how, he was yanked up and accorded superstar of the megachurch status. However, enough of these phony false prophets, along with their counterfeit monoliths, have had time to be tested, and they're being "weighed in the balances, and art found wanting" (Daniel 5:27).

To further illustrate the seriousness and sadness of this evil and dangerous innovation plaguing Christendom, a young pastor went to a State denominational departmental director and asked this question: "Whom can you recommend for me to pattern my life and ministry after?" The leader (?) in a high place with great authority advised his inquirer to learn everything he could from a certain pastor, whose church was in a growth explosion and was the talk of the town. But before the struggling neophyte could make his first appointment, the model admitted to having an affair with a church member and left the church.

I share one other (of the many) Faker, who rose among us. His church began to grow by leaps and bounds, and before long, he got himself elected president of his state convention. The state Baptist paper was reporting on him continuously, making the reader exclaim, "What kind of wonder is this?" Well, my wife and I had the exalted privilege of hearing him at a denominational evangelism conference. The music raised us to a high pitch, and then Mr. Sensation was introduced by the pastor of the largest church in our association (who, I was told by a former staff member of his, built it by secular means and by never rocking the boat). The long, elaborate, disgusting introduction helped decrease the high pitch the music had set, and then the speaker's fifteen minutes of jokes pretty well brought the temperature down to subnormal, which agreed with his simple sermon, delivered with no unction whatsoever. He was soon promoted to a larger, prestigious church in the heart of a city, but soon struck out and moved away. He hasn't been heard from for quite sometime.

However, **size** has become the trademark of this large denomination. When a member thereof approaches one of another church, **the first question asked is "What size is your church?"** I've heard that question asked over and over!

Such a concern is unscriptural and not a prerequisite to greatness. Jesus said, "Where two or three are gathered together in my name, there am I in the midst of them" (Matthew 18:20). Jesus chose to be born in a small nation, a small town, of small parentage (as the world considered the matter); chose small people as His apostles and associated with small people while He walked the earth. Size, as far as God is concerned, is no factor in ecclesiastical greatness. That is a concoction of man.

The denomination under examination remains the biggest by shallow, naive evangelism and by letting no one out, once they are members. Church rolls carry the names of deceased members, members of other churches, members who let it be known they are no longer interested in being on the church roll, and even members who have requested the removal of their names from the membership roll, but have been ignored. Why does such a practice continue with never one modicum of concern being shown by anyone in the churches or the denomination? The only reason I can think of for such incredible indifference is a desire to keep

70

the number one position, as to size, among Protestants. But much of the claimed membership is on paper only. It may look good in print, but the figures do not reflect the truth.

One of the first things I would do in each new pastorate (even within this denomination) was to try and bring the membership roster to meaningful and workable reality. As I would investigate and search in various ways to put a face with a name, I found encouragement nowhere. In fact, I encountered opposition. On one occasion, three (spiritually weak) men hemmed me up in a Sunday School classroom and told me to leave those inactive members alone and go get someone else!

This malpractice is a great hindrance to the work of a church. It encourages a nonserious attitude toward the true purpose, well-being, and work of the Lord's forces on the rest of the membership. Such tolerance turns the congregation more toward a social club than an army, equipped and eager to serve in the Lord's cause against sin and the devil.

The Nose Count

Another measure of greatness in this group is the amount of annual additions to the church, which along with other statistics are placed in directories of wide circulation. This emphasis is especially true on a regional and state level. Since preachers, as well as lay people, have a certain amount of pride, considerable pressure is placed on the clergy to produce a respectable number of additions--by baptism and transfer of letter--each year. This unscriptural test of a scriptural command, that of evangelism, generates anxiety and the temptation to cheat on the part of both "the cloth" and the laity in a local church. Why? In order to "keep up with the Joneses" and not lose face (as a success) with the populace and the brethren.

Affirmation of this perplexity came to me both at the beginning and end of my forty-five years as a pastor. My first exposure produced within me startling surprise; the second one resignation to the facts.

A dear preacher, pastor of a church in a sizeable town and near retirement, and I stood in the churchyard of the Concord Baptist Church. As we visited together, suddenly this dear man said, "I have such a burden on my heart. It is almost time for the fall, annual report to the association (denomination), and I have very little to report by way of additions." I had never dreamed of that being a factor for embarrassment because additions to our Lord's kingdom are not basically in the pastor or congregation's power!

My second exposure to the same type of remark came just before I retired from the pastorate. A fellow pastor said to me, "It's almost time for our association to meet, and I'm so ashamed to face the brethren with the report of my church's few additions."

I replied, "John, we do our best and leave to God the rest." I could say that because my church was reporting no additions by baptism. It wasn't because I was not preaching, praying, visiting; the reason was that the church I had inherited recently was in no condition to give birth. I was "killing myself," however, to change that. Oh, I could have baptized some folks, but it would have taken pressure on my part, with the ones I had in mind, and I did not care to put children, who were not ready for it, into the church. Neither did I want such to be on my conscience nor my record (with God). Just because there always have been, always will be cheats among us is no justification for my being one.

Staff search committees, especially those looking for a pastor, have heightened the temptation to pad because of a common practice by them. When a candidate for the office is being considered, one of the first things the committee does is to consult the statistical directories to see what kind of a production record that leader has in the place of his present employment. The delegation is looking namely for three things: number of annual additions, number in attendance, and number of dollars of annual income (for local and denominational purposes). It's called, "playing the numbers game."

Further illustrating the denomination's part in promoting this numbers game is the caption that appeared in the *Baptist Standard* May 17, 1995 (in red ink): **"First, Dallas, led '94 baptisms with 1,211."** Joel Gregory, in his book, *Too Great A Temptation* (The Summit Group, Ft. Worth, Texas, 1994) speaks of additions in the First Baptist Church, where he pastored briefly in the 1990s, and beyond. His contention is that Billy Graham began the Respondent Criterion of Success, i.e., religious worthiness is determined by the **number** of respondents to the invitation (to become a Christian) at the end of a worship service. In fact, Gregory indicates that it is even a measuring device of the preacher's power, effectiveness, and worthiness. Furthermore, he boldly states that additions to the church in Dallas, while he was there, were predetermined before the church service was even conducted. He reports that all of that had been taken care of the previous week by people being lined up to join. He did not say who did the lining up, but my guess would be that it namely was the large staff of the church. Anyhow, Gregory vows that the message and the messenger had nothing to do with people coming forward at the end of the preaching to unite with the church. He proceeded to say that he could have read the stock market report and there would have been the same **number** of additions!

Neither Jesus nor the Bible make response to the gospel a mark of a minister's success. Response to the message is not his responsibility. His duty is faithfully and truthfully to declare the message God has put on his heart. That's all! However, this is not saying that the messenger is unconcerned about response; he is. But it's not his role to push, or to feel a failure if there is not much or none.

Not everyone responded to Jesus, the rich, young ruler (Mark 10:17-22) being an example. Multitudinous others also rejected Christ and His message, but the aspersion was on them, not on Him. Two things about Jesus clearly stand: He never pressured and He never lowered the requirements! William Carey, dubbed the "Father of Modern Missions," faithfully served God and truth eight years in India before he witnessed one responding convert. The practice of counting noses as a requirement for ecclesiastical success, on any level, is an invention of man and not a heavenly standard. How in the world can a person profess spiritual enlightenment and not see the truth concerning kingdom operation and success!

The Nickel Count

Another degenerative measure of man as to church greatness is the amount of money raised (or contributed) each
year, especially for denominational (or cooperative work)
projects. Many Southern Baptist churches contain members
who are faithful tithers (a practice that is scriptural and
commendable), but SBC giving doesn't stop there, by any
means. Three offerings annually, above the member's
tithe--for state, home and foreign missions--are expected
and vigorously promoted. In addition to tithing and giving
to the Big Three, the SBC member is asked times without
number for other contributions. It all adds up to quite a
sum to be reported abroad in the annual report from the
local church.

But is even that a mark of greatness and automatic qualifi-
cation for heavenly rewards? Not per se. The poor widow
(Mark 12:41-44) gave only two mites (one source says two
pennies, another that the two mites equalled one-half of a
cent), but Jesus said she had given more than any of the
contributors, including those even who were rich, in that
she had donated all she had, even all her living. Jesus
pointed out in this instance that it's not the amount given
but the spirit in which it is given that really counts with
God.

What is my point? Giving to the right cause in the right
spirit is meritorious, but the grading and the rewarding of
such should be left to God, not to man. The small church
with the small offering might, in the sight of the Heavenly
Bookkeeper, be adjudged the winner among all of those
participating. Illustrating my charge that unjust emphasis is

being given in this matter of local church contributions to denominational causes is a headline on page fourteen of the *Baptist Standard*, March 20, 1996. It reads: "GREEN ACRES, PARK CITIES GAVE MOST IN 1995!" The first paragraph of the article says, "Green Acres Church in Tyler led all Texas Baptist congregations in total dollar contributions to the Cooperative Program unified budget in 1995." Later in the report, the amount given by the two churches is listed at $566,072 and $538,075, respectively.

Also, the giving to denominational causes through the "Cooperative Program" of every church--through its respective association--is listed in the state paper (at least in Texas) periodically for the month and for the year. In addition to that, each church's giving to its local association (for that aspect of denominational work) is reported (for the month and for the year to date) in the associational monthly paper, mailed throughout the association to local church staff members.

COMMENT

Outright sin and unwise promotion have (in my opinion) greatly tarnished the church and biblical truth in the last half of this century. Secular thinking and action have secularized the church, putting devotion to a denomination (no matter what it is or what it's doing) ahead of loyalty to God and the Bible. And I do not believe the two (denomination and God's cause) are, necessarily, synonymous. I also believe giving is a private matter--both individually and ecclesiastically--and should not be publicized either for bragging purposes or to exert pressure on people to give or give more. Let's let the Holy Spirit do the prompting.

SIX

PREPARATION

I left the First Baptist Church of Nash, Texas, in August of 1951, with two of the four children my wife and I had prayerfully planned for. The third child, Rebecca Lynn, would join the family the following February 20, 1952.

I enjoyed working for the Lord and with the people of the Nash church, but with seminary training lying ahead for a twenty-six-year-old, I felt I should get on with it. A fellow minister gave my name to the Farmers Branch Baptist Church, as it was then called, and after appearing before the congregation twice, I was given a strong vote to become the pastor. Though Farmers Branch, with a population of over 35,000, is well known today, this village, contiguous to Dallas at its north city limits, claimed a total of 900 inhabitants in 1951.

The church's selection of me to become its pastor was accepted, and I enrolled at Southwestern Baptist Theological Seminary, Ft. Worth, Texas, the largest of Southern Baptists' six seminaries. I would graduate in May of 1956 with a Bachelor of Divinity degree, having received the fourth and final child, Eva Diane, into our family the previous month, April 20, 1956. When Belva June Combs of Jacksonville, Texas, and I discussed our family plans, we felt led to set the number at four, never dreaming that the Lord would favor us with two sons, then two daughters.

Despite our having to endure some nasty comments, we stood our ground and deliberately carried out our plans. One lady remarked, "Brother Carraway hangs around the house too much." We shrugged it off because we knew what we were doing. We have never regretted bringing four wonderful children into this world. They have been a blessing and have added six precious grandchildren to our lives.

However, attitudes like the above further strengthen the conviction that our society, even in the church, is off the track of truth. God said to the first married couple, "Be fruitful, and multiply, and replenish the earth" (Genesis 1:28). Is not the (unjustified) nullification of this command selfishness and sin?

Sneering thoughts, silent or uttered, bespeak disdainfulness toward a married couple (usually a young one) bringing children into the world, thus having a family. To so think is to reject holy writ. Psalm 127:3-5 says:

> Lo, children are an heritage of the Lord: and the fruit of the womb is his reward. As arrows are in the hand of a mighty man; so are children of the youth. Happy is the man that hath his quiver full of them: they shall not be ashamed, but they shall speak with the enemies in the gate.

SEMINARY LIFE

I not only enjoyed but appreciated my seminary days, soaking up everything "thrown at me" to the nth degree. I heartily agree with the saying, "A call to preach is a call to prepare." I will confess to feeling that a seminary degree would make me more attractive to a church, but I definitely wanted the knowledge and expertise that such a degree would indicate more than I desired the diploma. I loved the Lord devotedly and wanted to represent and serve Him in the best possible manner. I enthusiastically accepted Paul's admonition, "Study to shew thyself approved unto God, a workman that needeth not to be ashamed, rightly dividing the word of truth" (II Timothy 2:15).

But this attitude is not shared by every man of the cloth. One day as a fellow seminarian and I lunched at a chicken resturant in Ft. Worth, we were groaning under the heavy load we were carrying. I'm not sure either of us felt certain we would hold out through graduation day. With that in mind, I spoke up, "Well, if I don't graduate, I will be grateful for the help received here that will enable me to better do the work to which God has called me."

He flashed back, "Bunk! If I knew I wasn't going to get that sheepskin, I'd quit today!" He soon went to a bigger church, then became director of one of the largest associations in Texas. He also was the one who laughed at a waitress when she, with a circular tray of ice cream, fell to the floor.

This experience--along with many others--caused me to lose faith in the denomination, because it gobbled up and utilized jokers like this one time and time again.

But in the seminary, I do not remember a single course I did not eagerly absorb. Ofttimes I was up until 2:00 a.m.

getting my lessons, putting my very heart and soul into each of them. After forty years, I still have every term paper, assignment and class note and refer to them frequently. Not all, by any manner of means, but many of them have an "A" on the front page.

THE CHURCH

I realized then, and even more later, how fortunate I was not only to be allowed the privilege of further schooling, but to have a good and growing church to pastor. It was at this church, to its credit, that I had my most supportive group of people. The deacons agreed that I was staying loyal to the scriptures and held up my hands, as did Aaron and Hur those of Moses (Exodus 17:8-16), time and time again.

The Fat in the Fire

After I had been in my new place of responsibility, as well as opportunity, several months, I could not help noticing that six deacons of the church had not attended even one of the monthly deacons' meetings. In addition to that negligence, about all these supposed-to-be leaders were doing was warming a bench. I knew we could never meet the demands upon us as a church, nestled in the midst of a population explosion, with that kind of indifference on the part of the membership. And that membership could, and probably would, be influenced--pro or con--by the example of the church staff and deacons. Since it is not so much what one says in challenging people but what he does, I felt I had no choice but to make a bold move. Following this talk with myself, I presented the delicate matter at our next deacons' meeting. My approach was, "Brethren, we are asking some men in our church to do something they prefer not to do, that is, being deacons." Not one of the men could claim disability as a factor. The deacons present, a solid group of Christian men, suggested that a committee from the deacon body be selected to go with the pastor to discuss the matter with each of the men in question. The visits were made, and it was unanimous for not serving. With that in mind, we prepared our report, suggesting that the church relieve them of this responsibility. However, before the next business meeting, the wives of two of the men who wanted the honor of the office for their husbands but not the obligation, stirred up a hornet's nest. Said they to their spouses, "That preacher is trying to throw you out of the deacon body and we're not going to let him." In other words, they were saying that they'd do as they pleased, whether the church liked it or not.

The six men, with their wives, were all present at our next monthly business meeting. The deacon recommendation that the six men be released from the responsibilities of a deacon was presented and passed by a large majority, but not without some opposition from one of the men in particular. When he rose to his feet objecting, I looked him squarely in the eye and said, "Are you willing to fulfill the duties of an active deacon in this church?" He refused to answer, so the vote was taken, but not without a backlash of three other deacons resigning, making a total of nine. We never missed them as the church geared for the challenge of a growing community. The stirred-up opposition caused some concern but was never able to prevail against the pastor. This was because of stalwart men and women of God standing for truth and progress.

81

His Bed; His Way

A report that I've never confirmed came to me that a neighboring pastor remarked, "Well, Carraway made his bed and he's going to have to lie in it." I didn't find my bed, wrapped in the approbation of God, uncomfortable at all. However, I do disagree with the pastor's alleged statement. I didn't make my bed; I made God's bed. He was the one who wanted done what was done.

I was told by a pastor friend that the pulpit search committee that led the church to call him had considered me. They went to the associational director for an evaluation. He said, "I think Carraway likes to have his own way." Though I had a better church than the one taking a look at me, still I was hurt by that statement when I heard it. No one could have been more cooperative with and supportive of that man than I had been. Furthermore, I was not interested at all in having my own way, but I did insist on God having His way in the church and work for which I was responsible and accountable to Jehovah.

How You Gonna Turn That Building Around?

As our community grew, so did the church. I knew that other Baptist churches would be coming to our area, and since the name "First Baptist Church" carries weight with people looking for a church home, I suggested that we rename the church "First Baptist Church." This was a legitimate step because the church had been the first Baptist church in that community for a long time. The recommendation was approved and appropriate signs were prepared and placed in strategic places. As the membership and attendance increased, so did the need for additional and larger facilities. This was begun by a brick nursery building, followed by a brick parsonage (heretofore, the church had rented a frame house for the pastor and family), and then the stage was set for a new auditorium.

Architect Adam Bliss of Dallas designed a pinkish-red brick, 600-seat building with a balcony and church offices and library/conference room across the building's back side. It would replace a well-worn and used auditorium, with a seating capacity of about 275 and would sit north of it, facing the pig-tail street, leading off of Valley View Lane, a main artery in the town. The enigma of the building(s) placement was that, with all the acreage just back of the one and only original building, the house of worship was hemmed in by residential houses and a very narrow street. No one had ever thought of cutting a street through the property owned by the church at the rear of the two-story, all-purpose building.

It was a Saturday afternoon and I was in my study (an improvised Sunday School classroom) at the church. Lawson Lewis, the town's mayor, paid me a visit. "Preacher," he said, "I've heard of the new auditorium you folks are on the verge of building, and I have a proposal for you." I had no idea what it could be. The mayor, a very nice and highly respected man, proceeded, "If your congregation will face that building east instead of west the city will pay for a four-lane parkway, with esplanade, at the end of which will be the new proposed city hall." What a dream, but at the moment, that was all it was. If, for any reason, the promised parkway did not become a reality, the large, new building would be facing a pasture and its backside would front the pig-tail (and only) street coming south from Valley View Lane. Of course, such a misplacement would make First Baptist Church, along with its pastor, the laughingstock of the entire Dallas area. It was a big step of faith (or folly) to do what the mayor was asking us to do.

When Mayor Lewis approached me, we were ready to start building the new church edifice. In fact, materials were on the grounds and workmen were beginning to move into position. Starting construction on the new proposed city hall building was several months away, yet I was assured that, if First Baptist Church would donate the land, the church's future buildings would be facing a spacious parkway and not a narrow passageway. The church's acreage that would be left on the east side of the parkway would be ideal for much-needed parking.

The city's proposition to us was relayed to the church, which, after considerable questions and discussion, voted to trust the city council's promise and start the building--facing the pasture!

In the days that followed, the new building at First Baptist steadily developed, but there was no sign of any kind of street in front of it. Passers-by sincerely thought "those Baptists" had lost their minds. And the devil seized the opportunity to bedevil and discourage the shepherd of that flock. He did it through a middle-aged couple, who were sitters. They were benchwarmers at church; they were porch-sitters at home. Most of all they were skeptical discouragers. Whenever, wherever they saw me, they would mock, "How ya gonna turn that building around, Preach?"

Then they would jeer, "There ain't a gonna be no parkway!" In their needling, they were calling the city council members liars and frustrating a thirty-year-old pastor. Each time they "pulled my leg," I would run--sorry to say--to the mayor for reassurance, which he would insistently and patiently give.

But finally hallelujah time came! I'll never forget it. One morning I happened to look out my church study window just in time to see a large earthmoving machine pull onto our pasture from Valley View Lane and pull a big hunk of earth into its huge scoop. **It was one of the most beautiful sights I have ever seen!** And work never stopped until the attractive William Dodson Parkway (named for a late and supporting citizen of the community) was completed.

On the house-filled dedication day of the lovely and spacious auditorium, the parkway in front enhanced it no end. My joy knew no bounds, but I was mortified, deep down in my heart, for the way I mishandled the heckling.

My Naiveness

By this time, I had been a preacher/pastor for some ten years without thoroughly realizing the true nature of a church congregation. Though I was a rookie in my Lord's work, I personally knew Him (beyond doubt) and was dedicated to following His way and will in my day-by-day lifestyle, regardless of what or where. My assumption that all church members were full of God and His love tripped me up over and over. Sad to say, but some members were empty, stingy, nonprogressive, hateful, envious, and a pain in the neck. Looking back to that era in my life, I can recognize how some church leaders saw this fact, causing them to play chess with members of their flock. I admire their wisdom (as Jesus did that of the unjust steward of Luke 16:1-8), but I abhor their continuing to accept the condition without trying to change it. How did Jesus handle the matter as He mixed with the kaleidoscopic throngs of people? He disdained the hanky-panky (of the scribes and Pharisees, for instance), quickly declaring the truth and applying it. Jesus taught and sought to bring them from darkness to light; He did not just go along with their erroneous thinking and conduct.

One example of the "chess playing" I mentioned is the rotation of deacons. Why would anyone want to set up a merry-go-round system like that? Are there that many men in the average church body who fit the qualifications of Acts 6:1-3, viz, that of character, spirituality, and wisdom? Doesn't rotation necessitate the ordaining of men to the deaconship, qualified or not? It grieved me to see those who wanted the office for the wrong reasons doing more harm than good when they got it.

Another sorrow of my heart was/is seeing prominence in the church based on social clout, not that of Jesus-like spirituality. Socially-minded leaders make a secular organization out of a spiritual one. When they're in control, you can count on a condition of spiritual shallowness.

Still another thing that is censurable among Christians is human pressure instead of Holy Spirit leadership. I saw this done in one of my pastorates with sad results. A man, grossly unqualified, was pushed into the deaconship by two deacons, without the right and authority even to approach the man, but all he ever did was cause trouble.

A NEW ASSIGNMENT

After seven years at the Farmers Branch church, I moved a hundred miles southeast to the First Baptist Church of Winnsboro in lovely East Texas. The year was 1958. The church was in dire need of a new sanctuary (or auditorium), for which architectural drawings had been approved and $40,000 raised. Nevertheless, the advance had stalled, the pastor left, and the pulpit committee searched eleven months for a new leader. When I was contacted, the new place of worship was emphasized as a priority need, and when I saw the church house, built in 1908, I agreed.

I had the church vote twice on my being installed as pastor. I now know the reason. I had come to realize that I was out of step with many so-called Christians, a situation I had not realized when I entered the ministry. The fact is, my move was not only facilitated by the pull of a new pastorate, but by a spiritually-weak and worldly church member in the church I left. I should have ignored his suggestion to resign (because of that support group I mentioned), but, foolishly, I didn't. The man was not qualified, to any degree, to advise pastors.

I accepted the call from this East Texas church, but before moving, I drove there for a meeting with the pulpit search committee. As I walked down a street of the town that morning, I met a man, influential in the church for the wrong reasons, and we exchanged greetings. After a brief period of general conversation, he moved closer, put his hand on my shoulder, and said, "Now, preacher, don't try to build that building when you get here." He proceeded to contend that children's voting had carried the issue, but that the majority of the adults was against it. Of course, he was lying, and I knew it then. I reported his words to the search committee, most of whom were on the building committee, and suggested that we have the congregation vote again on the matter. The vote was by ballot, unsigned, but we did ask each participant to mark his/her age bracket. As suspected, the vote was a strong one in favor of the new building with a large majority of the voters marking the adult bracket.

This building experience was quite memorable. There were many decisions to make, on which I had the congregation vote. That considerate and fair maneuver is still talked about--with appreciation--today by various members of the church. The cost of the structure (1960) was $189,000, $75,000 of which was raised before construction. The borrowed remainder was paid off in eight years.

SUMMARY

This chapter has covered ten years of my experience of serving God among churches, during which time I also was privileged to earn a theological degree. The two, school and hands-on experience, were vital cogs in the wheel of preparation to serve my Lord approvingly.

TEMPTATION

After three years in Winnsboro, I moved to the Texas Gulf Coast to a 1,200-member church, the largest, numerically, of my pastoral career. It was there that I had a similar experience to that of Jesus in His temptation by the devil, as recorded in Matthew 4:1-11. My experience was almost my undoing.

My Gulf Coast tenure of seven and one-half years got off to an unusual beginning. One was the call; the other was the moving.

A woman who had met me at the Farmers Branch church gave my name to the pulpit search committee of her church when it became pastorless. The committee came, heard, and called (that is, it wanted to recommend to the church that I be called as pastor). I heard, considered, and declined even though I was under the pressure of one man where I was (who was the kingpin of the church and community). As mentioned earlier, he began bucking me at every turn because I had challenged his leading in a particular thing that I believed harmful to the church and its image. I would take the same stand again. However, at the time, I felt he would have my job in six to twelve months. My friend (?), who had given my name to the committee, wrote me of her disappointment over my having turned down the committee's invitation to visit the church in view of becoming the pastor. I replied this way: Have your committee continue to hear all the prospects on their list, and if they do not find the man among them, they may contact me again for my further consideration. My terms were exploited. The chairman of the committee called me immediately after getting my word, urging me to visit the church, which my family and I did receiving of course royal treatment. I received a unanimous call and prepared to move.

Since the church from which I was departing owed me a week's vacation, I resigned, then took the vacation from which I would return on Sunday night, take Monday to finalize moving preparations, and the moving van would arrive at my house on Tuesday morning. The two men with the moving company found it more convenient to arrive bright and early Monday morning, which was a great inconvenience to my family and me. Oh, how some people do disrespect and manipulate the preacher to their own advantage.

The van's arriving one day sooner than it was supposed to created a problem for my family on both ends of the line. We were breathless at the end of the day when the truck was loaded and ready to roll. Then we arrived at our new home at two o'clock the next morning with no place to stay. Of course, you always find a way in such situations.

The new place of service was with a church with its two front teeth knocked out. It was on twenty acres of land, on which it had built a large complex of connected buildings back from the street without a permanent sanctuary. A temporary one, which was adequate, was provided, but the one-story, spread-out labyrinth with covered walkways running this way and that looked more like a public school than a church. The auditorium that would be centered in front of this "wild inextricable maze" would not be added until many years later.

Candidly, this church, along with the others of the town, was a victim of circumstance. The predicament in which this congregation found itself was due to a change in the demographics of the community. While steady growth was being enjoyed, this particular church had outgrown its location. Yet about the time the acreage was purchased and a most visionary building pattern was laid, the population began declining as people moved to higher ground even within the same county. Therefore, the steady flow of expected people into the new and elaborate expansion did not materialize. Instead of membership increases, the churches of the community began showing decreases in their annual reports. This created problems for the pastors among worldly-minded people who counted noses (new ones, especially) as a mark of success, not on their part, but on that of the parson. For instance, when I was later axed by this church, the personnel committee chairman said, "We don't feel that the church is making, under your leadership, the progress that it should!" I thought to myself, "Who in the world are you to judge?"

But my family of six moved into the new and spacious parsonage sitting on the twenty acres. We were the first family to occupy the part-brick dwelling of four bedrooms, a study, a large area for the living/dining room combination, a den, kitchen with built-ins, two bathrooms, a utility room, storage, and a two-car garage.

A TENURE OF SEVEN AND ONE-HALF YEARS

I was with this church seven and one-half years. I was very happy working for my Lord in caring for His flock, as He had instructed in the Bible and by His prophetic call to me. The children all settled in at school and church, and I was very busy in local, community, and denominational levels of work. June, though a busy wife and mother, became a vital part of the church and enjoyed her lovely, new home in a nice section of middle-class people and only three blocks from a well-developed shopping center. It was by far the nicest house in which we had ever lived.

During this tenure I was president of the local Ministerial Alliance, serving two terms; was a member of my denomination's State Executive Board, flying to and fro for meetings in Dallas; was invited to conduct my quota of "revival services" in sister churches; and was engrossed in shepherding the flock.

I stood by every surgery of a member of the church, sitting with the family in the family waiting room until the doctor appeared to apprise us of the operation's success and the status of the patient. I did this in self-reproach over a member of a former pastorate dying on the operating table in my absence. Though no one ever rebuked me, I chastised myself, vowing, so help me God, it would never happen again. A worldly family in the church criticized me for this practice, saying they did not want me there with them (a preference I honored, of course), but I knew what I was doing and why. Pastoring a church is a demanding occupation. The phone often rings day and night. Vacations are delayed, and sometimes even canceled. Desires of the pastor, and his family, are set aside in deference to the church family by the *dedicated and tender-hearted preacher.*

Pulled This Way, That Way

I had not been in this pastorate long when I discovered there were problems. Members began pulling on me to act contrary to the scriptures. The church was composed of two kinds of people. They were the outright defiant of truth and socially-minded and the more spiritual, right-acting ones. However, even the more orthodox would not stand with the pastor against a complaining member, even though he/she was wrong. This handcuffed the shepherd, rendering him powerless and without recourse.

The Vance Havner Week

The earthly highlight of my ministry, however, took place in this church. Vance Havner, a Southern Baptist evangelist from North Carolina, was with us for a week of services. I was starry-eyed, feeling that I had offered my people the very best. But the worldly ones in the church--and there was quite a contingent of such--did not respond to him at all.

First, they disliked his looks. He was not their image of greatness. Havner was a short, thin, frail person with very little hair on his head. He wore glasses (naturally, at his age of seventy), and there was even a nasal twang to his voice, but the little man was a mental and spiritual giant. Granted, the worldly crowd in the church, because of my publicizing the "man with the message" so vociferously before he arrived, was visualizing our guest the only way

93

of which they were capable--that of a worldly, human figure. They expected a dynamo of human beauty and strength on the order of Apollo and Hercules with a deep, resonant voice and riding into town on a white horse. They rejected him because he did not fit their (worldly) picture of greatness; I accepted him on the basis of his spiritual and moral attractiveness. It all depends on how you look at it!

In my fifty years as a preacher, I have met and/or heard some admirable servants of God, but Havner gets my vote as the best of all I ever met and heard personally. Author of thirty or more books, which were never thick, his preaching was filled with the Word and right to the point-- and the heart. Neither were his sermons long, but every word was power-packed to give his hearer a full meal. Nobody had to tell one of spiritual discernment that he'd been to church when this North Carolinian was doing the preaching. He blessed the godly; he infuriated the ungodly!

Havner Challenged in a Service

On Thursday night of the Havner week, the evangelist preached on "The Lordship of Christ," nothing new to the born-again child of God. At the conclusion of the message, he asked all who would to stand and simply say, "I confess Jesus Christ as my Lord." I counted it a privilege, and nothing out of the ordinary whatsoever, to be the first to say those words. Others followed, one after another, until a weird and heretical member of the church stood to his feet and said to Havner, "You have no right to ask these people to do what you're asking them to do. No one allows Jesus to be Lord of his life, and we should never sing the

song, 'I Surrender All,' because no one does, can, or will."
Very kindly, the leader of the service replied, "But you
want to surrender your all to the Lord, don't you?" The
recalcitrant defiantly said, "No, because it's impossible to
do."

I held my breath while awaiting the seasoned servant's
reply and handling of the matter. His reaction was master-
ful. Without raising his voice, he calmly said, "I think the
people in this service know what we're doing; who will be
next?" The testimonies continued.

The twice-a-day services from Sunday through Friday
closed; our music director, Dale Vance, and I drove the
Havners to Houston, where they boarded a train to Dallas.
I saw my admired brother in Christ the following Monday
night at the Texas Evangelism Conference in Dallas, but
never again. Both he and Mrs. Havner died and went to
heaven quite sometime ago. I look forward to meeting
them--and their kind--in "that pearly-white city." Won't it,
indeed, be wonderful there!

Brother Havner was invited for a return engagement at
our next business meeting, but Satan stopped that. It's not
a shock to hear that worldly church members don't usually
attend the midweek services. Soon after the invitation to
Brother Havner was voted (by those in attendance), a
deacon called for an appointment. He came right to the
point, "I understand that Brother Havner has been invited
to return for another engagement by the church." "Yes,
unanimously," I answered. "Well, we don't want him. He
was supposed to be preaching to the sinners [who said?],
but he preached to us." I silently thought, "Brother, he was

95

preaching to sinners." So at the next business meeting, we rescinded the invitation. I was glad I had not informed this dear man of the church's action--and I never did.

Sickness and Termination

Without warning, illness struck my wife. Her first symptom was vertigo; then an eye began to cross. After several physicians failed, a specialist in Houston diagnosed her as having multiple sclerosis. I was not familiar with the disease but was told by the doctor that it was incurable and fatal. She would continue to worsen, then die in about twelve years, he said. She lived fifteen. I did not tell June all that the doctor said, but while she was in the hospital for diagnostic confirmation, I told it all to the church. That was a big mistake!

From that moment, the worldly ones (the majority) determined to get rid of us. **Such a thing on the part of people claiming to be God's children never crossed my mind.** All six of us had been in good health with nice looks when they wanted us, but as I've been saying, they were devoid of the Christian graces (action speaks louder than words, remember). So, now that there were blemishes on us, we lost our standing with them and they kicked us out. **Only one person in the church, a godly woman, openly and persistently fought what was done.** A few others mildly resisted the butchering of a preacher and his family but were soon corralled with persuasion and threats by wolves dressed in sheep's clothing. There is no way to describe how this injustice and brutality affected my family and me, the pain of which lingers to this day. It's a horrible thing to experience. I think almost incessantly on how much worse the treatment of slaves or the atrocities of the Nazi holocaust were, and my heart goes out to the victims. How, oh, how could anybody or anything professing to be civilized stoop to such barbarianism and absurdities.

I was given orders to resign in December of 1968 and fought it until March of 1969 when I saw that further resistance was useless. My resignation stipulated severance pay and the use of the parsonage until the children were out of school. Our older daughter, a high school junior and vice president of the school's prestigious female marching band, returned to finish her senior year and graduate. We will always love and be grateful to the late Hazel Jeko, who let Becky live with her and finish that last year of school.

Where was Brotherly Love?

I have very little use for most of the preachers I know. Why would I say such a thing? Because, amidst my ordeal and since, they have turned their backs on me. That is not brotherly love and neither is it what God and Jesus commanded. I have no respect for or desire to be around anyone who thumbs his/her nose at God and His rules. One shallow preacher, who is tied more to his denomination than he is to God, dropped me like a hot brick when my wife became ill and I was barbecued by hypocritical church members. Not only that, but he had the audacity to ask a pastor and wife who lived about a mile from me at the time, while attending *religious* services at the SBC assembly at Glorietta, New Mexico, "How many jobs does ol' Bill have now?" I don't know what the couple, whose paper I threw each morning, said, but the number at that time was three. **God did, does, and will take care of us.**

ADJUSTMENT

The deadline for our remaining in the Gulf Coast parsonage came three months after my forced resignation with no job offer and no place, in particular, to go. It was reported by some of the church members that I turned down two churches wanting my services, but that report had not a smidgen of truth in it.

I did work briefly, during the three-month interim, in the welding shop of one of the refineries, then tried my hand at selling life insurance, but my emotional state would not permit my concentrating on much of anything. During this time of personal turmoil, I took and passed the state life insurance exam for my license. How, I'll never know!

Denominational Silence

Another thing I learned from this new experience was the inexcusable unconcern of the denomination in reference to the unjust slaying of a servant of Christ, who had been faithful to the Word and to the organization through which he served the Lord. Though the denomination was known to discipline pastors for dereliction of duty in leading the church to do its mission work through denominational channels, it never did one thing when a pastor and his family were unjustly and cruelly terminated. There was no investigation, no reprimand, no chastisement of a group that would brazenly stoop to such an un-Christian act, and no hand of help extended in any way to the slaughtered preacher. That which makes this report even more reprehensible is the fact that it's happened to many others, a percentage of which have even left the ministry.

Time's Up; Get Out!

June 1, 1969, was the deadline for our remaining in the parsonage. One of the members, who walked daily, would pass our residence and each time he caught me, he would ask, "Have you found a place to move yet?" I don't know just how he meant it, but I do know how I took it. It was rubbing salt in a festering sore.

But the moving deadline stared us in the face and I had to do something, so act I did. A moving van was engaged to move us to Texarkana, where my wife's parents lived, and we got busy packing. Packing day was a sad one as I went through every movement zombielike. Several from the church lent a helping hand, among whom was an out-of-town lady, visiting one of the volunteers. She later remarked that she felt like she had been to a funeral. I've often wondered what, under the circumstances, she expected.

In the late afternoon of packing day, my wife and children left by car for Texarkana. I would remain overnight and come with the movers. While lying on my bed, in deep depression, the phone rang. It was the ringleader of my firing inviting me to his house for ice cream. Did I accept? What do you think! However, that does bring up another puzzle in the matter we're discussing: How in this world can people be so ignorant of human feelings to think that they can abuse a person and still retain him as a friend! Nevertheless, I've witnessed the expression of this mindset often in my life as a minister. This very church that brutally threw my family and me out put heavy pressure (to no avail, of course) on me several times to return for special occasions. And they just could not understand why I flatly refused. Some folks are naive, indeed. Would a wronged divorcee be interested in attending the wedding of her ex-husband? Nonconsent to such overtures is quite understandable. Only one, stripped of all honor, decency, self-respect, and feeling, could respond.

Our temporary landing strip was a small, brick house in Texarkana, next door to a self-service laundry. Our residence was far too small for our family and belongings. The previous renters had kept dogs, with fleas, inside the house, a nuisance we were unable completely to eradicate. Another inconvenience was no stove the three months we were there. The house did not have one and the parsonage we had left, had a built-in.

Still in shock over what had happened to us, I tried hard to navigate normally, but the strength just wasn't within me to do much. I worked for a short time at an ice house, then got into life insurance selling with a Shreveport, Louisiana company. After training, I began working with Ernest Hall, general agent, out of the company's Texarkana office. The next several months were the most difficult of my life up to then. I floundered and felt out of place because I was not doing what God had called me to do. I also was not doing what I had been well trained to do. In late August, however, I was called to the pastorate of the First Baptist

Church of Fouke, Arkansas, fifteen miles south of Texarkana on the highway running through the town to Shreveport, Louisiana.

THE AREA'S WHIPPING BOY

Depraved human beings insist on practicing inhumanitarianism, which is more of a stigma on the offender than on the offended. It is a cheap and heartless act to make sport, which is disrespect, of another person. I understand that mature thinking considers the act a mark of inferiority on the guilty one who has to degrade others in order to feel any sense of worth himself.

Fouke was, unjustly, the whipping boy of its area. The village proper had a population of some 300, but people coming in from the surrounding areas made it seem larger. As true with all places, there were both the commendable and the uncommendable in this Arkansas community, and I found it no worse than other places where I had lived-- even in Texas. Yet from a natural view, it was the last place, probably, to which a preacher would want to go because of its lack of prestige.

However that may be, beggars can't be choosers, so the chance to move to the community, classified by many of the Texarkana area as backward, was appreciatively accepted by us. Of course, we had gone through a six-month conditioning period--three on the Texas Gulf Coast and three in the small house in Texarkana.

The church hired a van to move our furniture to the parsonage, which was a far cry from the one we had just left.

There were three bedrooms, two baths, a combined living and dining room, a den, a kitchen (with a stove the exact color of our refrigerator), and a double-car garage. The house was right by the church house to its north side.

We soon learned that there were some very fine and dear people in Fouke the five years we were there. Yet in my Texarkana luncheon club, I continued to be hurt by jibes about the place where I lived and worked.

I was now something I had not been before, a bivocational preacher. I had a church and I sold life and health insurance. I had been in the ministry twenty-three years and was forty-four years of age. I didn't make much of an impression as a pulpiteer, even at Fouke, in my early days with the church, because of my emotional state. But in time, that began to change as I adjusted to my new way of life with new friends and acquaintances.

The major thing accomplished during my pastoring days at Fouke was the renovation of the auditorium/educational building with a basement, all under one roof. The edifice of plain, cement blocks was bricked and refurbished throughout, at a cost of approximately $25,000. The money was borrowed from a member of the church, the county judge, at eight percent interest, and was repaid in a reasonable time without any problem.

OUR OWN HOME

Even though we appreciated the Fouke parsonage, we longed for our own home. Having sold a cabin on an acre of land in the Corinth community near Denton, we put the payment in a savings account, adding to it as we could. Three years after moving to the Texarkana area, our house fund contained $10,000, which was the equity my boss wanted for his home on Highway 59, five miles out from Texarkana. He was moving back to his place near Hughes Springs, where he owned a grocery store. The Atlanta Savings and Loan Company, Atlanta, Texas, allowed me to assume his $17,000, fifteen-year loan, with monthly payments of $155. The loan was paid off in nine years.

The house was brick with three bedrooms, two baths, living and dining room, den, kitchen, utility room, storage room, and a two-car garage and sat by the highway on an acre of land with a creek running through the backyard. The six of us were beside ourselves! We finally, for the first time in our lives, owned our own home. I remained with the Fouke folks two more years, living at our place and commuting to the services on Sunday and Wednesday nights. Then I accepted a call from the First Baptist Church of Rodessa, Louisiana, thirty-five miles from my house, which turned out to be my longest pastorate. I was there nine years.

My wife's condition continued downhill, and it finally became mandatory that she have round-the-clock care. By this time, diabetes was added to her multiple sclerosis. I placed her in the best nursing home (at the time) in Texarkana, where she resided the last nine years of her life. The children and I did not discard our family member; we sought for her the attention her condition demanded. I've never doubted our doing the right thing. June had a nice, semiprivate room with a telephone, TV, her comfortable chair, and a considerable amount of company. The children were attentive to their mother, and I tried to visit her daily, supplying anything she required or desired. also, when the children came home for the holidays, Mom was brought to the house for the special occasions.

After seven years of selling life and health insurance, I accepted a job as sales representative for a steel firm in Texarkana. Texas, Arkansas, and Oklahoma constituted my territory. I had appreciated my insurance experience, but the pressure required to get one to sign the application and pay that first premium got to me. I have never been one to apply pressure to another intentionally, since I disliked it being done to me.

Insurance of all kinds is a worthy and interesting business, but it's known as an intangible, and intangibles, not required by law or otherwise, are difficult to sell. From my seven years of selling it, I remember that everybody believed in it, everyone wanted it, all planned to get it, but none wanted it today! Yet if you did not get the application signed and the first premium collected, you had nothing--and neither did they. While a life underwriter, I graduated from the LUTC's (Life Underwriters' Training Council, Washington, D.C.) courses in personal, business, health, and disability insurance with classes meeting at Texarkana Junior College. Also, I qualified in every contest the company conducted but one. These contests were a constant happening, with the ones reaching the qualifying quota being wined and dined at a special place picked by the company. I even won one of those competitions by writing a total volume of $435,000 in business during a period of six weeks. Not only had my office been in one of the most imposing buildings in Texarkana, the State First

National Bank building but also I drew commission checks monthly for several years from the business I had placed on the books. The insurance business was very good to me. I have--overall--pleasant memories.

THREE JOBS

By the year 1974, I had three jobs--a church, steel selling, and a paper route. In '74 I had taken on a paper route, delivering 750 *Texarkana Gazettes* each morning, a job I kept for nine years. I would arise at 2:00 a.m., seven days a week, 365 days a year, crank up my Ford pickup truck, go to town for my papers, and was usually back home by 6:00 a.m. Then at 8:00 a.m., I began my traveling job with the steel company, five days a week. I conducted services at the church on Wednesday nights and Sundays, spending the day on Sunday at the church.

I have been often asked, "How were you able to hold down three jobs at the same time?" My answer: "By carefully organizing my time, not wasting a single minute." What was so wonderful about my employment was that it gave me little time to fret about my plight. It paid the bills and put a lovely and deserving daughter through college, qualifying her for a most successful career in on-camera television.

SUMMARY

The time period of this chapter is fourteen years, a time in which quite an adjustment in lifestyle had been made. The acceptance of going from a full-time to a part-time pastor, which was my calling, was not easy, but one must live with reality and make the best of it. No, those days were not a picnic, but, thank God, they were possible, and I learned, along with the Apostle Paul, that "I can do all things through Christ which strengtheneth me" (Philippians 4:13).

DISCOMFITURE

"And Joshua discomfited Amalek and his people with the edge of the sword" (Exodus 17:13).

Welcome to one of my favorite passages in the Bible, that of Exodus 17:8-16. I have preached from it many a time. The word "discomfited" is an interesting one. It is found only nine times in the Bible, always except once in connection with a mighty victory given His people by God. The word "discomfiture" is listed only once in the Word (I Samuel 14:20) and it, too, is connected with a great victory over the enemy of God's people (a race known as the Philistines). It is a victory again accredited to God. The word "discomfited" or "discomfiture" also attracts me as being special because I do not ever remember hearing it used by anyone of our day and time.

For the above reasons, I chose this word "discomfiture" to describe a great defeat in my life because I drifted away from God. I blamed the previously shared heartaches on others; I charge this one to myself. I have stated that the words "discomfited" and "discomfiture," in the Bible, relate to noble victories by God's children except one reference. It is preserved in Numbers 14:40-45. Because of faithlessness and cowardice on Israel's part, God refused to be with them in battle against the Amalekites and Canaanites. Even Moses would not engage in the fight. Both he and

109

the ark of the covenant "departed not out of the camp," but the self-willed and stubborn insubordinates rushed into the fray, only to be "discomfited" (Numbers 14:45) by the ruthless enemy. Their defeat was their waging war without God. So was mine.

A FOOL'S PARADISE

As 1983 dawned, the Carraways were in good shape. 'Tis true that wife and mother was no better; in fact, she was worse, but she was being cared for, and that was all we could do. The two sons had served hitches in the U.S. Marine Corps during the Vietnam War and had escaped injury. Don, the older of the two, was at the battlefront for two terms, in charge of a mortar cannon and he survived several close calls. Don was now a crop-duster, and Ron served on the Texarkana police force. Becky was happily married and living in Houston. Diane was a *PM Magazine* co-host at a television station in Waterloo, Iowa, where she was quite successful, with five of her programs gaining national recognition and use. She also met her future husband, Ed Piette from Detroit, Michigan, while in Waterloo. They had a lovely Texarkana wedding New Year's Eve of 1983.

And I too was doing well. My three jobs were under control, my income was adequate, and I was living comfortably. But a three-pronged storm was brewing!

Don left his job at the Red River Army Depot, where he worked on tank transmissions, in May for a crop-dusting assignment in the state of Washington. There was no way he could be kept out of an airplane. Flying was the love of his life. Realizing that opposing him in his chosen vocation was useless, we often discussed twofold safety, i.e., a reliable aircraft and being in the pink of health when in flight. Don's violation of the first mentioned necessity cost him his life at age thirty-four.

A Fatal Plane Crash

My beloved first-born was a maverick and a daredevil. He was a maverick in that he was a nonconformist; he liked to do his own thing his way. Don was not good at following a prescribed curriculum, but he was unbeatable in thoroughly learning his craft, whatever at the moment it might be. He was a regular patron of the available library, checking out stacks of books on that which he was studying at the time. He was a skilled carpenter, competent electrician, proficient lapidist, and capable airplane pilot. He could also play the piano and guitar--well, after a sort.

After completing his crop-dusting commitment in the state of Washington, he made an unwise decision--buying an experimental (self-made) aircraft and attempting to fly it to Texarkana, Texas. (I knew nothing about such plans.) I have reason to believe that the plane was far from reliable, a possibility I think Don also was aware of. But as I said, he was prone to court danger, taking far too many chances.

He took off on Saturday morning, June 4, 1983, and made a fuel stop in Oregon, where he also had a ham sandwich and coffee. A phone call by the *Texarkana Gazette* to his stopping place revealed his conversation with the airport's attendant. Don said to him, "The plane is not handling well

111

today, but if I can get home without killing myself, I plan to work on it." Soon he was airborne again, reaching northern California at Lake Shasta near Redding in the afternoon. He planned to visit a friend in Fresno that night.

Some teenage boys from a nearby detention home saw the plane circling the area repeatedly, but it disappeared and they thought nothing further about it. The next morning (Sunday) they were rattlesnake hunting up a small, scrubby mountainside when they discovered a crashed airplane upside down, with the dead pilot strapped inside. The boys, after taking the money from Don's wallet, got in touch with the sheriff's department. The body was not removed until Monday, which means that decomposition had already set in because of the hot sunshine and high temperature.

From the identification found in his moneyless wallet, the county coroner began calling the Carraways listed for Texarkana, Texas. He reached me on his second try, informing me of Don's fatal accident. Though hurt, I was not surprised or shocked. I had known for sometime that such a thing could happen and had even taken out a life insurance policy on his life, just in case. He had walked away from two crashes already, but his third one was his last.

Calmly, I asked the coroner what steps should I take, and upon his advice, I called East Funeral Home of Texarkana. Its personnel took over from there. After the mandatory autopsy, my son's body was prepared for burial and flown to Shreveport, Louisiana, arriving on Thursday night. The following afternoon, Jim Adams, Don's pastor, conducted the closed-casket funeral service, doing an excellent job.

His having gone through the same experience, in the death of a twelve-year-old son, helped him relate to and comfort us. Interment was in Chapelwood Cemetery, Nash, Texas, and a veteran's plaque marks the grave.

The following Monday morning, I drove to DFW Airport and caught a plane to the crash site, accompanied by my brother-in-law, Doyle G. Combs. I had to see for myself the plane in which my son died and exactly where the crash happened. Collecting Don's personal effects from the coroner, we flew home the next day. By the way, the billfold, empty of any currency, aroused suspicion of theft by the sheriff's office, and upon being questioned, the boys confessed and surrendered the money.

Another Death

Two months to the day later (August 4, 1983), my dear wife, June Carraway, age fifty-five was discovered dead in bed at 2:00 a.m. I was working my paper route, a route unknown by most who knew me, and was not found to be notified until 5:30 a.m. The body could not be moved without my permission.

June was born to Hollace and Leatha Combs, June 15, 1928, in Mount Pleasant, Texas, the first of two children. The family, joined by Doyle Glenn, later moved to the town of Jacksonville, Texas, to work with Jacksonville College and the First Baptist Church. That was where I met my future wife in May, 1946. We married February 1, 1947. June Combs Carraway was a beautiful and lovely person. She played the piano flawlessly and was a good wife and mother. We looked upon her fatal illness with a deep sense of sorrow and regret, something that turned our family completely around. June's funeral service was conducted in the East Funeral Home's chapel, as was Don's, and her body was laid to rest also in the Chapelwood Cemetery of Nash, Texas. My body, upon my demise, will be placed by her side. The inscription on our bronze marker reads, "In life we sought dignity; in death we seek heaven." I felt that wording was sufficient as a testimony to our children and grandchildren.

When the shepherd's family is diminished in any way, the wolves in the church, go to howling and biting. They take the frustration of their wickedness out on the pastor's family, whom they never loved in the first place. They'd really like to beat up on God, but since that is impossible, they do second best by taking their vengefulness out on His called, separated, and true-to-the-Word servant. For a *man of God* to try to work with many so-called churches of today is to take his life in his own hands. The reason for this condition in the church? The absolute abandonment of church discipline by the church of today.

Regardless of how the Gulf Coast church meant it, the brunt of its senseless and unjustified action was borne by my wife and the mother of my children. That was the most confusing aspect of all in our literally being thrown out of the church and the community. Mrs. Carraway had done no harm to anyone (neither had I, as far as that's concerned). Yet she was thrown out, without mercy, to the wolves. But upon her death, here came a letter of sympathy signed by many of the members of that church (?)--an overture that I felt was hypocritical and contradictory of their demeanor the past fifteen years. What they did to her when she needed their love, prayers, and help was an egregious, sinful act by those claiming to be the redeemed of God. And the fact that they've never shown any sense of wrongdoing, just strengthens my accusation. Not one time in the twenty-seven succeeding years has one person of that group admitted guilt or asked forgiveness.

My Big Blunder

On September 12, 1983, Meghan McDermott, was born in the city of Houston, becoming my second grandchild. My first was Bryan Paul, son of the late D. B. Carraway. It was my joy to play grandma for most of a week, helping an incapacitated daughter, Becky, at the birth of her first of three children. I enjoyed every minute of it and would have stayed longer if the "kids" hadn't insisted that they could then handle it.

By late 1983, I was a one-job operator. My employment at the steel company fizzled when a hard and wide-spread economic crunch hit. I was the last of three outside sales representatives to be terminated. I had decided that I had thrown papers long enough (nine years), so I resigned from that position. Now, all I had left was the church.

An Interpolation: I made a costly mistake in charting my educational preparation. Yet if I had known that it would ever be necessary for me to have "an emergency landing field," it would have been hard for me to enter the ministry in the first place. I never dreamed even once that I would ever find myself barred from full-time church work. Therefore, I prepared myself, vocationally, strictly for the ministry. I did not even bother to consider the how-to courses in education that would have qualified me to teach school. So when I was forced to go bivocational, all of my secular jobs were at the entry level. That is why I always had several jobs at the same time.

Since I was now down to one job, I looked around for an additional and new one. I had become resigned to being able to get only selling jobs, some of which were on a commission basis exclusively. I tried over and over to get some type of government job, but never had the proper pull or connections. Those jobs, it seems to me, are obtained by who you know, not by what you know. Am I wrong? If so, advise me.

The job I took came about by buying a particular product. I wanted the best in its field, and after testing the machine, strongly felt that I had it. I applied for a job where I had bought this appliance and was hired immediately since it was a commission-only position. Even though it was a door-to-door selling arrangement, I was so sold on the product myself, I felt sure I could sell it to others. And if I had been under the right supervision, I honestly believe I would have done well--real well.

But I did not have a good boss. Neither was he a good man, nor an adequate trainer/leader. Each employee paid him $300 for the product up-front. The retail price of the item was $629, which allowed an adequate profit to keep a sales person in business, if the full retail price was received. One thing for sure: one cannot stay in business unless a fair and reasonable profit is earned. Despite that fact, which our employer should have known well, we-- believe it or not--were encouraged by the management to give the very worthy merchandise away. He baited the salespeople, about ten in number, with poorly constructed prizes, promising higher standing with the company, and eventually a lower wholesale price for the commodity. He would often say, "If you walk out with fifty dollars, or even less, you've got more than you had when you walked in." What kind of entrepreneurship, pray tell me, is that!

The few weeks (very few) I was with the company, I was the biggest frog in the pond. It felt so good to walk into the sales promotional meetings each morning at 9:00 o'clock with the biggest report. But, I restate, most of the time I was giving the product away, and, in reality, going up (or maybe I should say down) fool's hill. The afternoon I decided to quit, I had called on a neighbor, who had just bought one of our items from another sales team. He voluntarily told me what he paid the two young men for it. Same old story: they too were giving the articles of merchandise away; they, like me, were not selling at all.

The following morning I checked in my inventory and bade farewell, but not without getting a bawling out from an infuriated exemployer. Sometime later he died, I am told, at a rather young age from a rare blood disease. His son, who also was the victim of his father's tirades, now, with his mother, runs the business.

About the time I began the work just described, I had also started a bargain house and used car business, but that too was a big mistake--and a disaster. Three things were its downfall: lack of experience, founding it on credit, and depending on the buying public to make it a success. It did

117

not take me long to see that I had better stop proceedings and the growing debt at the bank, bailing out the best I could. I had no alternative but to sell my home, and make some changes in my pattern of life.

Looking back on that dreadful scene, I suppose the avalanche of stress and strain finally got to me, causing me to lose my mental and emotional equilibrium. Also, I wasn't as close to God as I should have been, a fact that caused blindness of judgment and vision. Candidly, I was fed up with being bossed and hurt by worldly church members and bad bosses, so I closed my eyes and leaped, right into a "heap" of trouble.

Before that, my home was paid for; I had no debts; I had money in the bank; my wife, whom my children and I had watched beaten to death by a cruel illness, was in heaven; and I was now foot-loose and fancy-free. And I had great plans--business, personal, and social--but they didn't, necessarily, include God. For a short time I was living in a fool's paradise, but though my wheels were spinning, actually I was going precisely nowhere.

When the full reality of my predicament hit me, I got sick. I lost my thrust, my interest in life, my social desires, and my appetite. In a short time, I lost twenty-five pounds and none of my clothes would fit me. Now that my forward progress was static, I began going over the past several years of my life, marveling that God hadn't killed me. I had neglected Him and His precepts, and I also recognized something else--that I was at His mercy. During the latter months of my dilemma, I worked at a convenience store across the highway from my house. But everything I did was by rote--without feeling, excitement, or joy. Neither the company nor the customers had any idea of the turmoil through which I was going, but I'm sure they knew something was wrong. For the most part of my employment there (at minimum wage), I worked the night shift, which was from 11:00 p.m. to 7:00 a.m. That gave me a lot of time alone to cry out to God, and my thoughts were filled with the life and misery of Samson (Judges 13-16). He was selected by God to be His servant and champion against the enemy of the Israelites (the Philistines) before he was even conceived. But Samson couldn't find sufficient satisfaction just being the Nazarite (separated unto God) God had called him to be. He was lustful, tempestuous, and revengeful--too full of self and the world to be all that His Lord meant for (and needed) him to be. Because of that, he was captured by the enemy (of God and his people), who put out his eyes, bound him with fetters of brass, and forced him to do the lowly task of grinding grain in the prison where he was incarcerated.

During those long nights that I toiled in an unsophisticated setting, I felt a parallel between Samson and myself. Seemingly, I too had been abased by the forces of evil from a lofty state to a menial one. Still I knew I would have to do my time in the clutches of that and those obnoxious to me. That is, I knew I was where I had no business being.

My deliverance was unique; it came through a robbery of the store! One day (April of 1985) I was working the afternoon shift, 3:00 to 11:00 p.m. As I relieved the manager, whom I had baptized into the First Baptist Church of nearby Nash, Texas, thirty-four years previously, a heavy rain was falling and customers were practically nil. Finally, the

119

two I was relieving left and I was all alone in an empty store. I felt so cozy and safe, never dreaming that I was about to be robbed at gunpoint. As the store's assistant manager, I was interested in the daily shift reports, so I took a look at the one just completed, over which I lingered several minutes. Even though all was still as a statue, something caused me to look up from examining the report, and when I did, I was looking into the barrel of a pistol. It looked like a .25 caliber automatic and was held by a young, black man with a woman's stocking over his head and face. I made no sound; neither did he. But the robber did point, with his free left hand, to the cash register and, of course, I got the point. I opened it and he, while holding the gun on me with his right hand, emptied the till of $430 with his left hand. Then he glided out as quietly as he had come in.

I had often thought about a store robbery, but assumed it would be during one of the two night shifts, probably the one from 11:00 p.m. to 7:00 a.m., the one, I usually worked. I had wondered, should I ever be such a victim, would I be shot? Well, I wasn't, for which I breathed a sigh of relief and thanked God. Then I called the sheriff's office and the manager I had just relieved. Soon the store was filled with police and company personnel, to whom I reported what happened, just the way it occurred. Nothing more, nothing less.

Despite my honest, unvarnished account of what took place, I was suspended during the investigation period, which lasted three weeks. First, I was required to take a lie detector (polygraph) test, which was a farce. After I had answered each question truthfully but unemotionally, the administrator of his own testing firm left me for quite a spell, finally returning with the company's security officer. "Mr. Carraway," he said, "the polygraph is acting strangely, indicating that you're not completely telling the truth." Somewhat of an argument ensued, concluded by his saying, "Why, my professional reputation is at stake in this."

I thought, but didn't say it, "Maybe so, Bubba, but my freedom is at stake in this." I did say this to the two men: "If you are telling the truth, I know something that you two do not know. The polygraph is not reliable."

Three weeks later, another security man took me to another office, had me sit in a room alone for thirty minutes; then returned to say, "What do you think should be done to one who would fake a robbery and pocket the money?"

I stood to my feet and replied, "I've had enough of the treatment I'm receiving. If you have any further questions, contact my attorney." After giving him my attorney's name, I asked when would I know whether I still had a job or not. He said that he would call me--one way or the other-- that afternoon. I'm still waiting for the promised call!

After waiting a couple of days for the call, I (in my own mind) quit, and got busy with more importantant things to occupy my time. I've passed that store many times, but I've never entered it since the day I was robbed there.

DECISION TIME

Earlier in this chapter, I referred you to the only time that the word "discomfited" is used in the Bible, depicting the defeat rather than the triumph of Israel, the people of God. (Numbers 14:40-45). Israel was overwhelmed in a war in which they fought without the assistance of the **I AM THAT I AM**. Because of weak-kneed, distrustful-of-God disciples, the Almighty did not assist them in their fight with the foe. Also remember that Moses, with the ark of the covenant (symbol of God's reality and presence), did not aid them either. They lost, not because God fought against them, but because He did not fight for and with them. That, to a T, describes my discomfiture.

It was in the sixth month of my ordeal that I came face-to-face with the sobering facts. I had a difficult decision to make, consisting of two parts. Would I rebel against God, going out into the world and the things of the world, or would I come back, fully with no restraint, to God and His ways? The decision was mine to make.

As I pondered my decision, I thought of the biblical account of Balaam of Mesopotamia (Numbers 22-25, 31:1-8), one who at least posed as a representative of God. However, he was not an admirable person, much less a preacher, and was executed by God's command (Numbers 31:2,8). Consequently, I positively believed that if I chose the way of the world as Balaam did I too would be destroyed. That destruction might come through me, or it could come from God.

Yet I also well understood the requirements of my alternative. I had been there--to my abuse, betrayal, hurt, and expulsion. Was I willing to wear the yoke, bear the cross, and feel the poke, press, prod, and prick of the goads again? Also, was I willing to meet God's insistence on an all-out commitment to Him, His word, His way, and His work? I am saying that God demands a full surrender of oneself to Him. If it doesn't come, God does not respond to that individual by working for and through him. For one to think otherwise, he is only kidding himself.

But I knew that when I did make that consignment of myself, I'd jump right back into the fire because, though there would be peace and even joy within, there also would be Satan-prompted enemies--in and out of the church--to face and fight.

With all of that in mind, I went to my knees literally and turned my life again over to God. I prayed, "Dear Lord, I ask Your forgiveness for my Christian inconsistency and if You'll re-enlist me in your service, I promise, here and now, that while I am one of Your shepherds, I will never do anything, anywhere that I wouldn't do if I knew my flock was looking." I sincerely tried in the seven remaining years as a pastor to live up to that promise.

HELP ARRIVES

Just before the roof had fallen in on me, I had reestablished acquaintance with a widow in Winnsboro, whom I had not seen in twenty-two years. While pastoring in her town, I became close, at least in my own mind, to the family because of a serious, even fatal, accident. R. E. and Anna Florence Johnson had one child, Jon Ronald, who was the only survivor in a three-person auto accident. The tragedy happened about three months after I moved to the Winnsboro pastorate and I conducted one of the two funerals. Ron spent a long time in the hospital and at home recovering for, though he lived, he was seriously injured. I tried as best I could to minister to the family during those days, days I never forgot. There were also other memories of this family because of even more pleasant associations with them. The late R. E. Johnson was a faithful deacon in the church and the vocational agriculture teacher in the Winnsboro High School for thirty-five years. His wife was active in her church, school activities, and the community.

It was she--and she alone--who befriended me in the days of trial and despondency, and no matter what I shared with her about my past that wasn't complimentary, she was not disturbed in the least. She also made it quite clear that she was my friend and cared what happened to me.

Ann, as I call her, and I married February 22, 1985, at her Winnsboro home on a Friday night, with rain coming down, lightning flashing, and thunder rolling. We had a weekend honeymoon at the Holiday Inn in Tyler, and I went back to work on Monday. We lived in Texarkana for a while; then I sold my home there, liquidated my indebtedness, and we moved to her place in Winnsboro. Now I had a dependable friend, a nonhostile community in which to live, and friends who would help me get back on the right path.

SUMMARY

My discomfiture of 1983-84 was a heart-rending, regrettable occurrence, but it could have been worse. It certainly taught me a valuable and lasting (I hope) lesson, i.e., always stay with God in love, obedience, and service.

CULMINATION

It was only a few days after settling in Winnsboro when we ran into Lee and Ruby Ramsour at the local Dairy Queen. Brother Lee was adroitly and resolutely reshaping a corny dog. I knew of Brother Ramsour from having seen articles about him in the *Baptist Standard,* the official weekly periodical of Southern Baptists in Texas, but we were not personally acquainted. He had married Ruby, an interesting and gracious lady, after the death of his first wife. Upon retirement from the pastoral ministry, Brother Lee had settled in peaceful Winnsboro to be near his daughter and son, Betty Reed and Evangelist Larry.

But Ann knew them both, so after greetings, we were invited to sit with them in their booth. They had just come from their last service for a church with which they had been associated. Soon as they learned who I was, they asked if they could give my name to the chairman of the pulpit search committee of the church they'd just left, Eaves Tabernacle, located in the Union Community near Leesburg and thirteen miles northeast of our town. I gave the go-ahead, and in two days or less was contacted. I agreed to conducting the upcoming Wednesday evening service and remember well my text. It was an expository treatment of Psalm 51:1-19, the repentance of David after his double sin of adultery with Bathsheba and the murder of her husband, Uriah. I seriously doubt, at that time, if I could have used any other scripture since that passage was tailor-made for my condition. Both my spiritual and emotional tides were at low ebb in that I felt very weak and unworthy. Of course, I did not knowingly make my present mystique known to my audience. I got through the message, my first in about five months, rather safely. The service seemed to go well, and I felt not only God's blessing, but a dab of spiritual strength returning. I was cognizant of the fact that it was the spiritual food and exercise I was getting that did it.

RESTORATION

In a few weeks the Eaves Tabernacle Baptist Church, named for its first pastor, voted unanimously for my being its pastor. The church, located very near two large lakes, was at the end of a pleasant drive down winding roads and beautiful countryside which we enjoyed for a minimum of three round trips a week for two and one-half years. As a bonus, the trip was often spiced with seeing deer.

The Eaves folks were a wonderful group, a pleasure indeed to work with. Ms. Emma Martin, a senior citizen, was the sweetheart of the church, and Ann loves to tell about their first meeting. We arrived for that first service a shade early, as I suppose preachers or speakers ought to do, and took a seat on the second row of pews on one side of the building. The two sections of pews were separated by a center aisle. Spotting a nice-looking gentleman across that aisle from me, I scooted over to visit with him. When Ms. Emma, as I felt comfortable calling her, arrived, she walked to where Ann was sitting and stopped. My wife spoke, then asked if she would like to sit by her. "Well, yes," she replied, "this is my seat." Each time the tale was told, we would react with an appreciative chuckle. We were glad Ms. Emma loved her Lord and had a special place in His house--and in the hearts of the people, I might add.

Nancy Anderson was our music director and her cousin, Carol Shelton, played the piano. Both were pretty, pleasant, and proficient. All of us enjoyed singing praises unto the Lord under their direction. The church, for a small one, had a good mixture of older and younger adults, young people, and children. It wasn't long until the church began to grow, with people of various ages uniting.

Lost On The Lake

Something happened right after our going to Eaves that rocked our community and church. A man got lost amidst fog on one of the already-mentioned lakes or in the woods nearby. Thankfully, he was rescued, and in time, many members of his large family united with the church.

A New Building Proposed

One business meeting night, a dear lady said, right out of the blue, "We need a building for the young people." She was the mother of two young ones, a boy and girl. I could have choked her, but instantly I knew she was right. We had good and nice facilities (an auditorium and fellowship hall), but we didn't have enough. We did need an educational building for not only the young people, but all the congregation. Yet, being human, I had not let myself think about it because I knew well, from experience, the rigor of a church building program. Be that as it may, I not only knew the suggestion was valid, but that I must support it. The church also responded in the affirmative, vital help was obtained from the Texas Baptist Architectural Department in Dallas, and plans were drawn for the building. Another wonderful thing happened: the Texas Baptist Men, a church-building crew who worked at no charge, agreed to build the building.

Bo Pilgrim Contributes

As we were raising money and pledging more, I felt inclined to write Mr. Bo Pilgrim of nearby Pittsburg, Texas, and for whom some of our members worked. In writing the letter, I assured him that he and I were the only two people who knew about my overture, and that if he did not care to respond, he and I would always remain the only two persons aware of the epistle. I simply said that I felt he might enjoy having a part in the project and suggested a $5,000 figure. He responded by return mail with a check for the suggested amount, for which we were all deeply grateful. Even though I left the church soon thereafter, today there stands on the Eaves grounds a lovely red brick building, symmetrically placed, for Christian educational purposes that gives the church adequate and balanced facilities for Christian service.

A CATASTROPHE

The church was growing in just about every way one could expect. Attendance and membership were increasing, the material aspect of the church was being improved, people of the area were looking our way, and we had just been the recipient of a Harmony-Pittsburg Associational award (plaque presented at the annual meeting) for the small church showing the most growth the past year. Also, I had been selected to preach at the next annual meeting of the association.

An Exciting Phone Call

In the midst of all these goodies, suddenly and unexpectedly, I received a call from a longtime friend in reference to his pastorless church. He, as chairman of the search committee, asked if I knew any prospects. I sent him the names of two pastors in our association, wished him well, and forgot the matter. Two weeks later, he called again, asking, "Would you be interested in the position?"

I had known this person for thirty-seven years. We met when I became pastor of his church and meshed right off the bat. Each had deep rapport with the other. Not too far into my ministry with his church, he surrendered to God's call to the ministry, or so he said, leaving the management of a department store business. His wife possessed a sparkling personality and his two young daughters were just about as cute as they come. Later, they would be joined by a brother. Having enrolled in college, he became pastor of a nearby church, doing a commendable job, and honored me with the privilege of conducting revival services there for a week. Those seven days were perfect bliss as we worked and fellowshipped together. After a tenure of some two years, my friend moved to another church, 500 miles away. There he went through a church fight, resigned, and returned to the business world, where he remains to this day.

Only through this person's phone calls did I learn of his church being pastorless. I had met the former pastor at a luncheon and liked him, his congenial wife, and two young sons. Yet a segment of the congregation, with the defection of the youth director, tried to terminate him. The vote did not bring the required two-thirds majority, so the dissenters walked out and started a church in the high school auditorium. This First Baptist Church was located on five acres of choice land in a town on the edge of an area that was growing by leaps and bounds! The opportunity to build a genuine New Testament church there was a temptation too great to resist.

However, if I had not been the victim of whacky reasoning, I would never have gone to that place. I assumed, and never even thought of questioning my assumption, that it was (1) a normal community, (2) a membership left who had stood by a man of God on biblical grounds, (3) a group who wanted to be led by the Spirit and the Bible, and (4) humankind of wisdom and kindly regard for their fellowman. Oh, yes, there was another piece of erroneous cogitation. This bedroom community was predominately made up of younger married couples with children. I licked my chops as I thought about what a help a pastor and wife, in an age bracket of sixty-two years, could be to these young adults. **Are you kidding?** Why, they knew everything. They asked no one for any help whatsoever when it came to advice. It was one of the most repulsive exhibitions I have ever witnessed in my life. Their thinking was sick, sick, sick!

As to number 1 (a normal community), it was not. It was the most pagan place I've ever had any dealings with. As to number 2, wrong again! The ones left had not voted, in retaining the pastor, for a man of God on biblical grounds; they had stood by a personality, strictly on a fraternal basis. When he left, so did their loyalty, i.e., there would be none for his successor. Concerning number 3 (those wanting to be led by the Spirit and the Bible), cross that one out also. They rebelled at being led (they would do the leading), they had no capacity for the Spirit, and they were not about to be obedient to biblical precepts. And now for number 4 (wisdom and brotherly concern). They did kooky things and would cut a throat, especially that of the pastor, in a New York minute.

I share here an example of their kookiness: The chairman of the finance committee would not deposit the evening offering immediately in the bank, letting it remain in the counting room all week, neither would he allow the report, including that of attendance, to be registered on the register board (for the membership to see) until a week later! That was a new one to me, one who had been in "it" for forty-two years. How can enthusiasm be promoted that way? So, discovering what was (not) going on, I counted the money, made out a deposit slip, and deposited the bag in the bank. The minute this well-employed businessman discovered what I had done, I found his keys to the counting room (his resignation) on my desk.

I made an enemy of the layman music director when I spoke with him about his buying six-packs of beer in the large supermarket and offending (a few) fellow members. Also, it was he who caused a scene in the first business meeting I moderated, when we hired a secretary (there was not one paid staff member when I arrived) and youth director. Jumping to his feet, he said, "If you're going to pay them, you're going to pay me!" Have I made my point? But never dreaming that things like I've recounted could take place by civilized (?) people claiming to be the children of God in a church of God, I took the job--much to my sorrow shortly thereafter.

An Unbelievable Scene

I appeared before the church twice before being called, not receiving one cent as honorarium or expense money. See, I had my head in the sand, even then. After preaching in a sister church, where the committee came to hear me, Ann and I met with the committee at its church. What we saw was a pitiful sight. Debris was everywhere. Roll after roll of carpet lay about, with no one to install it. Two beautiful doors, to replace the decrepit ones at the front of the auditorium, had been in a back room for over a year, and, repeating, there was no paid staff at all. Also, the offices were in shambles. There were no vacuum cleaners to clean the two buildings, one a two-story, and no mower to care for the five acres. Furthermore, the church had a heavy debt resting on top of it.

Despite all this, I appeared before the church in view of a call, with seventeen votes cast against me. I accepted, and Monday morning, my friend and his wife, who were realtors, went with Ann and me to find a house. The church had no parsonage but provided a housing allowance. At our last stop, we scored! It was a dream home, a model house with everything on an ideal site. We got a VA loan and moved in. The cost was $100,000, with monthly payments of $1,055, for thirty years. We would sell our home in Winnsboro, putting the proceeds therefrom on our new place. In accepting the church, I had promised eight years, then I would retire at age seventy. We believed we could have the house just acquired paid for by then.

Eight Months Down The Drain

Another reason I accepted this place of service for my Lord was because I have never been afraid of work. I like to work, not just for work's sake, but for results' sake. We locked up our Winnsboro home, moved, and went to work. Our first project was our lovely house. With Ann's brain and my brawn, it was soon put in a condition that was appealing to the eye and restful to the body. Then I concentrated on the church. I preached the Word, making no bones about my complete dependence on God for success. I also toiled with others as we painted, laid carpet, and put furniture where it belonged in an orderly arrangement. Day by day and bit by bit we put Humpty Dumpty back together again. After several months, the facilities sparkled and were the object of many kind remarks.

Almost from the beginning of my ministry there, I had begun working on and with the membership roll. At every pastorate, I tried to find the sheep, putting a face with a name and putting a body back into active service for the Lord. The membership roster, like everything else, was in a mess. I did this work practically single-handedly by writing, calling, and visiting. I soon learned that many on the roll were dead or belonged by now to other churches or were inactive and wished to remain that way. The rest of the church seemed unconcerned about the matter, considering it no problem. I thought differently.

A member of the church, a man, came to my office one afternoon and made a suggestion that led to my Waterloo, which I now sincerely believe was his intent. "Preacher," he said, "why don't we reunite with the group that left us?" He explained that the former pastor had caused their leaving, but now he was gone. Why stay apart? I replied that I would be willing to merge with the other church, but only if it could be a merger of equity. The two pastors would be copastors of the united body, and each side in reuniting would be treated equally.

My visitor left my office and went immediately to see the director of our association and former pastor of our church. The next day the director called me, suggesting that the other pastor and I have lunch with him, during which he presented the plan. About the first thing he said was, "One of you may have to leave, and maybe both of you." As we talked further, I mentioned the copastor arrangement as being the only fair one, to which the other pastor (the former youth director of the church I pastored, age 26 and single) replied, "I thought I would be the pastor. With your experience, you could be a lot of help to me."

After getting home, I thought seriously about what had been said at lunch and called the associational director, telling him that I was not agreeable to the merger unless it could be on a copastor basis. He answered with something like I should state my feelings and stand by them. Then I called the other pastor and told him the same thing. He said, "I'm praying about it." But he was lying and had already determined to do everything within his power to be the pastor and demote me to his assistant. He and his cutthroats had tried once to take over the church but had failed. Given another try, they wouldn't fail again. Under the leadership of our associational director, each church was to appoint a three-member negotiating committee to work toward reconciliation of the two bodies.

It was then that a traitor to me and the church stepped in. He was one of the sorriest human beings I have ever met. His wife, who asked for the job, was my secretary. He went to the other group and pledged his allegiance to it. This was necessary, in his being a traitor to us, because he had voted against them when they failed to fire the pastor. He, unknown to most of us, also went to the chairman of our negotiating committee and swung him to his side. The chairman, in turn, influenced the other two members to stand with him in making the other pastor the sole pastor of the amalgamated body. This was the recommendation formulated by the two committees and presented to me for approval. I refused to accept it.

A brief statement was prepared for presentation by the chairman of each committee to his respective church in an official business meeting. It stated that there would be no consolidating at this time by the two churches. The report was read to our church by the chairman of our committee, the other two members standing at the front with him, but then he made another report, most if not all of which was a falsehood. It berated me for not going along with the crowd and accused me of actions in the committee meetings that were absolutely and positively untrue. I was so shocked and taken unawares that I walked out of the meeting, leaving them to do as they wished. I knew I would never reenter that church building. My wife and I drove some ten miles to a Denny's restaurant, had sausage and pancakes, then went home. Soon the phone rang and it was our committee chairman offering me the same deal, by church approval, that I had rejected. Again I balked and turned in my written resignation the next day. We moved back to Winnsboro in a month, putting our house in the hands of our realtor friends, who never turned a hand to sell it.

The friends who got me into the boiling pot defected from truth to the winning and popular side, pledging their allegiance. It's easy to understand their motive, which was for business and social reasons. Six years later, the female of the twosome died suddenly at the age of sixty-two.

An Expensive Lesson

The fourth lawyer we contacted advised us to declare bankruptcy on the house, which we did. But it still cost us $22,500 to extract ourselves from such a predicament. The Veterans Administration did not lose one penny on the deal. The mortgage company bought the property at the foreclosure sale, getting the guaranteed $36,000 from the VA. The VA, in turn, bought the property from the mortgage company, getting back its $36,000. Then the VA sold the property to a couple on a thirty-year note for more than our note was. These facts are on record in the courthouse of that county and are open for viewing by the public. It is true that we, through the insistence of one man in the church, were given $12,000 severance pay, which makes our total deficit from the shellacking $10,500. The deceitful and conniving preacher went on to get his doctorate, then returned to the state from which he came.

REJECTION AGAIN

After returning to Winnsboro, we saw an advertisement in the state weekly paper of our denomination that attracted our attention and aroused our interest. A preacher and wife team was being sought to work with a Baptist church in Harrogate, England, composed namely of Americans, working at a nearby air base. We called the listed number, only to learn that we were talking with our state Baptist headquarters. From there, we were referred to our Foreign Mission Board in Richmond, Virginia, which would screen any applicants for that ministry.

Ann and I cooperated with the board's every requirement, giving references, undergoing examinations that were quite personal as well as thorough answering oodles of questions on voluminous forms, increasing our insurance, buying our passports (which we still have, unused), making a round trip of 270 miles for an interview with one of the board's examiners (of those being considered for foreign mission service), and being informed that our getting there and back would be at our own expense.

And after all of that, we were rejected. I asked the lady, who telephoned the board's decision, the reason for our application being turned down, only to be told, "The board never gives a reason for rejections." Stung by being declared unclean again by people much dirtier than we, I wrote Keith Parks, president of the FMB and with whom I had been a student at Southwestern Seminary, for an explanation. He not only declined to reveal the basis on which we were denied but showed no compassion and offered no commiseration whatsoever. I did not answer the

137

letter. In fact, I put the matter behind me and became interim pastor of a church not far away. However, when editor Presnal Wood, another seminary classmate, informed us in the *Baptist Standard* of Park's plea for clemency, I put the issue back on the table.

Parks, we were told, had asked the Foreign Mission Board's trustees to allow him to break the rules--the long-established rule about the president's retirement, that is. The rule was that the president would retire (from the FMB) at age sixty-five. Parks wanted to continue beyond that point. Wood wrote, "Let him serve!" I replied to the *Standard* editor, "Let him retire!" And I explained why. But that wasn't all I did. I wrote the chairman of the board's trustees of my objection to Parks breaking the rule and gave the reasons why I disapproved. Then I sent a copy of the letter to Parks as well as to certain influential personnel in the Southern Baptist Convention.

In my letter to the board's trustees, I charged Parks with lying. In the letter I received from him (and I have it on file), he contended that I had been told the reason(s) for my rejection. Of course, that was totally untrue. He continued to stand by his falsifying in his letters to the trustees, regarding my letter. I was gratified when the trustees denied Parks the privilege of continuing as FMB president. What is that scripture? Isn't there one about a person receiving judgment without mercy, who has shown none? Try James 2:13; maybe it's there. I had long presumed that those connected with foreign missions would be the kindest, most loving and most spiritual people to be found anywhere. Mrs. Baker James Cauthen, whose husband preceded Parks as the FM board's president, attended a morning worship service at one of my pastorates, impressing me with her cordiality and unpretentiousness. She was there with her missionary parents, Brother and Mrs. W. B. Glass, her father preaching the message. I thought all those connected with the Richmond place of service were that way. It was a tremendous letdown to learn that I was mistaken.

Ignore Him

Isn't there a hymn that says, "Crown Him, crown Him?" The world-in-the-church philosophy is, "Ignore Him, ignore Him!" Someone asked, "If Jesus came to earth today, how would people treat Him?" The reply was that he would not be railed at or imprisoned or crucified. He'd just be ignored! Would any church members treat Him that way? Yes, because many in the church are not saved, not born-again, and not children of God.

Allow me to share a case in point concerning what I'm talking about. In June of '95, my wife and I returned from Chicago and the American Booksellers Convention to have a phone call awaiting us. It was the director of an SBC association (of some twenty-five churches in an area not far away), who requested a copy of my book, *A Call To Faith And Morality* (BAC Publications, 1993). One of his pastors had read it, being impressed enough to want all of his fellow pastors to review it. But evidently he realized he wasn't free to act according to his own conscience (and he isn't). With that in mind, he contacted the associational director, who in reality is his boss, requesting his examination and approval of the book first. He knew he could quickly get into hot water, deep and fatal, if he

139

should be labeled a reactionary to the denominational plan, program, and procedure. He was unerringly correct. How well I know. By the same token, the director understood that he too faced the same penalty if he endorsed a disapproval of anything the denomination was practicing and/or promoting. Although theoretically, each church in the Convention is independent, sovereign, and free to run its own business, that is not the way, in actuality, it works. For it to be circulated that a pastor is not cooperating in the cooperative work is tantamount to putting out a contract on his professional career. He will soon find himself without any kind of ministry opportunity in that religious communion.

In talking with the director who called and whom I knew, I told him that he wouldn't sanction the book, but he insisted that I send it to him. So I mailed him a complimentary copy and received a thank you note quickly. However, eight months have passed without a further word. That is the tactic of my denomination, i.e., "Ignore him." And such a practice is unscriptural and unChristian. If I'm off the beaten path of truth, my Christian brother has the responsibility of helping me get back on it. If I'm on the beam of truth, then I should be commended and followed. What this brother has done to me is the equivalent of refusing to speak when spoken to, or more seriously than that, it is slapping me in the face.

There Is Coming a Day

In the fifty years that I've sought to serve my Lord in answer to His call for my life, I have never thought of myself as being on trial with any fellow pastor, denominational figure, or other critic. **They're on trial with me.** And when I fully see their mendaciousness, I turn away from such, knowing they are in error and are no model for me to follow.

I began my college work, rooming in the same dwelling as did another young preacher. He was a happy-go-lucky type with a slap on the back for everyone. He also smoked cigarettes. Finishing college, he went to a seminary, gaining a doctor's degree. It wasn't long before he began to rise among the brethren. He pastored his fellowship's larger churches, often spoke on the denomination's nation-wide broadcast, and was often the speaker on various occasions at different places. Yet, to me, he preached from the vocal chords up, not out of an anointed and burning heart. Years passed, then he called me one day. I learned from the call that I had just located near where he was, and he exuded goodwill. However, it was without substance, i.e., it withered as fast as it sprang up. I attempted to effect a meaningful friendship with him, but he was uncooperative. Finally, I dropped any effort of trying to relate to him and went on my way. A few weeks ago, his death at the young age (for today) of sixty-eight was announced in a newspaper. Though he was Mr. High-Muck-a-Muck in his adult, earthly life, I cannot help but wonder what his status is now, wherever it may be that he resides.

I am unconcerned about my image here as long as I'm doing my best to walk with God and according to holy writ, but I am absorbed with what my image will be in eternity. What that will be, I do not know. But I hope and pray it will be a Christlike one since I say with Pontius Pilate on at least one thing, "I find no fault in him."

TEN

A CHURCH IN DRY DOCK

My last church before my retirement was in paltry condition. Acting on the tip of a friend, I had called the director of the association of which this church was a member about a more-attractive-to-the-eye situation. He replied, "Oh, no, that's not for you, but I know one that is and will have no problem in getting you before its search committee." **Later I understood why. They were in no position to be choosey.** As it turned out, I believe he was saving the church about which I inquired, for another who, sub rosa, had been chosen to succeed him upon his retirement, which wasn't far away.

Nevertheless, I arranged to preach before the committee of the director's choice at a church near me, with whose pastor I had a good relationship. I preached from that favorite scripture I mentioned earlier, Exodus 17:8-16, naming it "Lessons Learned in Christian Service." Both the service and the meeting with the committee went well, and I was soon installed as the pastor.

From my first glimpse of the new field of labor, I knew I faced a monumental task. What I saw almost made me sick. The church was in ruins both spiritually and physically. One of "them" doctors had preceded me, leaving things in one heck of a mess. It was quite obvious that this "old ship of Zion" was going nowhere until she spent extended time in dry dock. But as I've already stated I was accustomed to this kind of assignment and frankly it bothered me very little. I found tremendous fulfillment in making something that was despicable an object of loveliness, admiration, and conversation. I practically lived in my

142

coveralls the twenty-two months I was there. It took me three weeks, working like a slave, to ready the parsonage for our moving into it. All property and facilities of the church had been neglected, and the educational building had been flooded, ruining all the carpet. During an ad-on project, the roof had been left off the night a downpour came. Upon finishing refurbishing the parsonage, the few helpers and I moved to the church proper. Far-flung painting commenced inside and out. I became well acquainted at the local paint store rather quickly. New carpet was installed; the nursery was completely redone; the most antiquated folding chairs I have ever seen in a building were replaced with new, modern ones; drinking fountains were added; and we even bought new hymnals for the auditorium.

An Unsolved Mystery

A deacon, who was also the treasurer, presented a riddle I have not solved to this day. His wife's wail over the deplorable state of their church's facilities could be heard above all others. He and two others had done most of the remodeling work, and upon my arrival, I jumped into the challenge with both feet. Just as I was beginning to help in bringing the situation out of the doldrums, this deacon and treasurer said to me, "Now, preacher, you're not going to be able to accomplish all that you desire while you're here." I let the statement slide, but I should have cornered him right then and there as to what exactly he meant. But I didn't have to wait long to find out. After we had finished a certain amount of the work to be done, he began dragging his feet and bucking me. But I knew what had to be done, and for the glory of my Lord, I determined to do it. Yet his attempt to discourage the leader and short-circuit the remodeling effort began getting to me. I was further aggravated by his coming into the auditorium while I was stamping the church's name in the new hymnals, and asking, "Preacher, what are you doing?" I told him, whereupon he said, "There's no sense in that." I kept silent, but I thought, "Gee! Thanks for the compliment!" Therefore, when he came into my office one day with his gripes, I was not abusive, but I did speak to him, calling a spade a spade. I also advised him that I'd be resigning soon. His wife, whom I had worked so hard to please, reported falsely that "Brother Carraway talked so ugly to Henry [fictitious] and Henry came home crying." **Moral to the story: The preacher, though beleaguered and pummeled, has no recourse, and is to take whatever harassment hurled his way.**

But the mystery I started out reporting in this section still remains. Why would a child of God, recognized and honored in the church, oppose improving God's property? Was it that he was afraid of the improvement program putting the treasury at a low level, necessitating his giving some of his own money? What did he give? I have no idea. But imagine people who claim to be born-again, heaven-going children of God trying to hurt and hold back His work. It just doesn't make sense!

Inflated Membership Roll

As usual I found the membership roster inflated and all but meaningless. The pastor before me, in order to make things look far better than they were, had many people on the roll who were not members and never had been. Some of them had attended Vacation Bible School or youth camp, or signed a visitor's card in a worship service, but they were not members of our church and did not want to be. I followed my usual custom of writing, calling, and visiting in an effort to find out who was who and what was what!

Unfit for Leadership

The unfit are determined to fit--into the running of the church. There was an incompetent but persistent couple among us who insisted on being the leaders, defying the pastor, and going over the heads of the deacons. The sad part about it is that they often got their way. The favorite maneuver of the male was, after having his proposal discouraged by the pastor and deacons, to propose it at the next business meeting. He was really the main reason I left.

Celebration Day

After laboring for many months, we finally got all the property and facilities of the Lord there in admirable shape. And we had a glorious Sunday of celebration.

RESIGNATION & RETIREMENT

I reached age sixty-five in December of '90 and retired *from the pastorate* June 1, 1991. I was tired of the hassle. There were too many complainers, resisters, and sitters and too few encouragers, helpers, and doers. It grieves me that the church is not a happy place now, at least for the spiritually-minded and those desiring to be loyal to the

Word of God. The reason? Too much in it that shouldn't be, and not enough there that ought to be. Plain and simple, that's it.

With deep regret, I confess that I have no desire or intention ever to pastor another church. I sincerely believe that a Bible-reading, Bible-following, real man of God cannot succeed or stay in the average church of today. I stated this to a denominational employee several years ago who vehemently disagreed with me, but I still stand by that contention. I've seen nothing since that would change my mind. The problem is twofold: irresponsible leadership and assertive, unqualified membership, each of which does not lead the church rightly, i.e., in the way Jesus would have it go.

God's Order

God's order of church leadership is that the flock (local congregation) be led by a shepherd, but he must be a God-called and incorruptible one. What an awesome responsibility is that of the pastor of a church! He lives each day under the awareness that God is holding him accountable for the way the congregation believes and behaves. In Ezekiel 34:10, God says, "I am against the shepherds, and I will hold them responsible for what has happened to my flock" (LBT). This is why God's leader must know the guidebook and faithfully lead the church under his care to conform to it. He is not lackadaisical but responds at once to the bleat of the sheep or the howl of the wolf. He loves the sheep because he loves the Lord, and he feeds and tends them in a worthy manner (John 21:16-17). This is why no person in his *right mind* would light-heartedly take on such an assignment unless he was compelled by his God to do so. When one truly understands the nature of the ministry as we call it, he has no desire to be a part of it, preferring the back instead of the front seat. The ministry is demanding of the shepherd in reference to his deportment and his performance. He lives in a glass house and any and everything he does, or doesn't do, is not only noticed but magnified. Also many congregations never forgive a leader who erred among them. Oh, he is to forgive them, but they have no responsibility to do likewise toward him.

Up to the time of my cataclysmal denouement, I declare under oath my striving constantly with all my heart to live up to "the high calling of God in Christ Jesus" for my life. Subsequent to that, I confess (as I already have) laxity and cause for criticism of my demeanor, for which God, as He promises (Hebrews 12:6-8), punished me.

But, I repeat, it is God's decision that His called servant lead the flock, not the other way around. Defiant, balky sheep, who disrespect and resist the leadership of a spiritual and trained leader, will not go unpunished. God will see to that.

MAY A PREACHER EVER RETIRE?

In this study of basic Christianity, I am trying to present biblical truths for all, but especially for those who will not probably study these issues in the Bible for themselves, but hopefully will read this book. For that reason, may I address a controversial subject, now that I am retired (only from the pastorate, not from God's will), on which I'm

147

hearing considerable discussion? I refer to the question: Should a preacher ever retire? Of course people thoughtlessly thinking and saying that are inconsistent, even with their own feelings. The current emphasis is on youth, not on senior citizens. The majority of congregations want a younger, not older, leader. If a pastor is never to retire, where is there a church that will call him at age seventy or beyond? Yes, agreed that there are a few, but I expect very few.

Notwithstanding our own surmising, what does the Bible teach on the subject? Admittedly, neither the preacher nor any other Christian is ever to stop loving, obeying, and serving God, but after a sufficient number of years in service as a pastor, that one has the right to retire from such a demanding duty. Let us hear what Numbers 8:24-25 says about it:

> This is it that belongeth unto the Levites: from twenty and five years old and upward they shall go in to wait upon the service of the tabernacle of the congregation: and from the age of fifty years they shall cease waiting upon the service thereof, and shall serve no more: But shall minister with their brethren in the tabernacle of the congregation, to keep the charge, and shall do no service. Thus shalt thou do unto the Levites touching their charge.

The work of the Old Testament priest had much manual labor in it; therefore, hard work, which took its toll. God never does that which is unfair to us; he expects no more than what is equitable and just. True preachers, as the priest type is called in the New Testament, are called of God and are loyal to God. Consequently, their life is not their own; it belongs to God and the people. This is why the Master sanctions the retirement of a preacher after he has served a reasonable amount of time in a most demanding vocation.

My Retirement

I did not have, or pursue 45 years in the ministry as a time to loaf, travel (abroad and to unnecessary meetings), receive a gift car annually, bank a big salary (my highest was $35,000 annually, and that lasted only eight months), cater to those who would constantly wine and dine me, soft-soap biblical principles in order to be popular with everyone, and be off the field more than I was on it. Why would I have fought a call like that! But God's call to the ministry is not that kind of summons. Frankly, when I did retire from the pastorate I was fatigued.

I have been retired almost five years, and **I love it!** Somebody might say, "Well, it puts you closer to death." That's undeniably true, but there's nothing I (or you) can do to change that. We must be prepared and trustful of God. Also it doesn't hurt to reread the scriptures concerning the death of God's children. According to the Book, the departure isn't repulsive at all!

My love for God has not diminished; in fact, it has grown stronger, as has my love for the Bible and studying it. I enjoy going to church, but it must be a reasonable expression of what the church is supposed to be. I do not miss preaching (though I'm ready anytime the call comes) since there are many other ways to serve the Lord and strengthen His body. Two of those come to mind quickly, which are leading the singing and painting the building(s), both of which I do where I worship.

Yet I must admit that I'm grateful for being relieved of the heavy responsibility that was mine as a shepherd. Yes, I still work because I am not one to sit and do nothing (and I'm not criticizing retirees who do). But I work that of my own choosing (remember that I claim a God-controlled mind and heart) and at my own pace, which is a lot easier.

RESUMPTION

Though I didn't resume what I left at retirement, there was the resumption of my vocational life in about three months. I launched a second career in a venue different from the one I had followed for forty-five years. It was in the field of writing/publishing.

Journalism seemed to have been within me at birth, but my training therein began with my junior year of college. I not only took my first journalism courses, but to say it again, I was editor of the college paper that year. I was surprised to hear that the writer of an article does not write the headlines, that being the prerogative of the editor. I was also taught the five W's of the first paragraph of every news article, i.e., What, Who, Where, When, and Why. "How" was a sixth requirement. Every report had to be written, so the first paragraph told essentially the whole story and could possibly be, on occasions, the only part of the submission for which the paper had room. I continued my journalism courses my senior year at a different school, and though I was not the editor, was a part of the school's newspaper staff. My two instructors were C. S. Boyles, Jr. (Austin College) and M. T. Andrews (Henderson University), each of whom paid me a treasured compliment.

Boyles autographed his faculty picture in the 1949 yearbook, *The Chromascope*, with, "Editor, you really did a

151

good job this year--I enjoyed working with you." He wrote Western fiction in his spare time.

Andrews said, when he returned the required journalism scrapbook, "W. B., I regret that an A is the highest grade I can give you for this excellent work." His gracious remarks humbled me, but I was the only student in the class that illustrated the book with drawings and special printing. Of course, these priceless mementos are kept in a safe place and referred to often.

All through my forty-five years of pastoring, I submitted many reports to the local newspaper and articles for various denominational periodicals. I do not remember a single time that my work was rewritten to any degree by the editor. I suppose that was because I had been taught to write properly.

In 1974 I wrote and published my first book, and I assure you I didn't know what I was doing. However, considering the circumstances, it turned out pretty well. It was a biography of Clarence Ballard Stanley, president of the Texas Baptist Children's Home (BMA) in Waxahachie, Texas, for thirty years. He also became my stepfather three years prior to his death, December 25, 1969, at age eighty. His five sons--Richard, Bruce, Ted, Dan, and David--paid the bill and I wrote the manuscript and managed the printing and binding of the 1,200 copies. As far as I know, all copies have been sold.

But these experiences constituted the sum total of my writing and publishing experience when I launched my second career in the fall of 1991.

LEARNING WHAT NOT TO DO

It embarrasses me to admit that my first several thousand dollars spent in the writing/publishing business was learning what not to do. First, I threw $300 in the trash can when I hired the advertised "typing professional" to typeset my first book. Her error-filled work was unusable, but I paid her in full and made an entry in the book of my brain. It was "Get a computer and learn to do this work yourself. Do not depend on another."

So in the fall of '91, with a bit of advice from my stepson, who has a computer science degree from East Texas State University, Commerce, Texas, I purchased an IBM compatible LASER 386 SX computer, a Hewlett Packard Desk Jet 500 printer, and a Xerox 5009 R/E copier. By following the manuals' instructions, I installed the three machines but had no idea how to operate them.

In March of '92, with only eight weeks of training on the computer, I ripped into publishing my first book, *A Call To Faith & Morality*. And my education in what not to do continued. Unknown to me until the book had been on the market for sometime, it was full of structural mistakes-- blunders, some of which I didn't even know were boo-boos. Out of the 500 copies printed (thank God, there weren't more), I had 150 left, which I stopped trying to sell. There went several more thousand dollars down the drain.

But that's not all. In working with the R. R. Bowker people, who market the ISBN number (International Standard Book Number), a distribution must, I tossed another

153

grand out the window. With no criticism meant, I was talked into investing that amount annotating my free entries in Bowker's *Forthcoming Books* and *Books In Print*. To my knowledge, those annotations never sold one book for me. However, my experience of learning what not to do is a common one. John Kremer, most successful in the writing/publishing field, tells in *1001 Ways To Market Your Books* the debacle of his first publishing effort. He still has 6,000 boxed books in his garage because the advertising and printing did not synchronize. Others, well established in the business now, tell how at the start they had to learn **what not to do.**

I GET A BREAK

My first book was read by a dear friend and member of a former pastorate in Nash, Texas. She had completed a course on writing one's life story and was interested in writing her memoirs. She offered me the job. By then, I was gaining in expertise but I found the undertaking almost overwhelming at times. However, we stayed hitched and produced *Daughter Of Destiny*, by Carlene Howell. The 286-page hardcover book with an illustrated dust jacket and a foreword by the former Texas governor, Ann W. Richards, is a beautiful production and marketing well.

Just as Carlene's book was coming off the press (or bindery, or manufacturer of my camera-ready copy), I attended a two-day seminar, conducted by John Fooks, columnist for the *Texarkana Gazette*, at the Red Lobster Restaurant in Texarkana. It was there I met Letha B. Smith, who was interested in publishing a genealogical-type book about her husband's family. There were five generation figures that would develop the narrative, Letha's late husband being the last one. John Gene Smith, before he died September 17, 1994, set aside money for telling the Smith story and got Letha's promise that she would publish it. When I met her in June of '95, she had the hand-written manuscript almost completed. We signed the contract September 18 and the books were in our hands by February 6, 1996-- about four and one-half months later. It's a beautiful work of 176 pages, three photographs, fifteen chapters, and a three-color hardcover in black, white, and gold. Several readers of the interesting and well-related story of slavery in Texas have remarked, without knowing others had done so, "This book should be made into a movie." Both Letha and I hope that kind of talk continues!

THE PUBLISHING FAMILY

When a newcomer to the publishing world prepares his first publication and applies to the R. R. Bowker Company for his ISBN number, he immediately lands on some important and helpful mailing lists. These veterans in the self-publishing field are looking for clients and Johnny Newcomer is seeking guidance and assistance. Each needs the other. The list contains publishers, publishing houses (to take one's camera-ready copy and bind it into an attractive book), printers, editorial services personnel (proofreaders, editors, language experts), book distributors, the wholesale houses, bar code people, and worthy professionals selling services that a rookie **must** have.

One of my first contacts at this point was with a man in Santa Barbara, California, by the name of Dan Poynter. It took him eight, long years to write his first book, which

155

was one on parachuting, but following that, Dan took off! He is now the author/publisher of seventy books and is highly respected and greatly used in the independent publishing world. I followed Dan's book, *The Self-Publishing Manual*, in 1992 while writing my first book and have ordered several other different ones since. It was quite fulfilling to meet Mr. Poynter February 17, 1996, in an all-day meeting of writers and publishers at the Adams Mark Hotel in Houston, Texas. His immaculate appearance, his tremendous knowledge of our trade, his calm and friendly demeanor and cleverness were refreshing to one who had not felt that way about some of the so-called (and self-styled) leaders among us.

His handling of a situation taking place on the Houston-bound plane the previous day was a classic, and an illustration of how to do it. Dan was seated by a gentleman who inquired as to his type of vocational work. Mr. Poynter replied, "I am an author and publisher," to which his neighbor said, "You don't look like one." The wise one from Santa Barbara countered with, "Oh, this is my day off!" Can you beat that one? The matter was settled, with no chance for rebuttal. It's easy to respect and follow a man like Dan Poynter, and I'm glad he got my name from the R. R. Bowker Company.

While attending a conference in San Francisco, California, in 1994, I met Tom and Marilyn Ross from Buena Vista, Colorado. They were my pick of all the speakers in that four-day gathering of publishing people. They too after many years in the self-publishing business, have written *The Complete Guide To Self-Publishing*, published by *Writer's Digest Books* (Cincinnati, Ohio, 1994), which was also widely used in publishing my second production, Carlene Howell's memoir.

TRICKS OF THE TRADE

Have you ever wondered why there are blank pages in the back of a book? I had--many times. Book pages are cut from large sheets of paper and put in signatures (sections) of eight, sixteen, thirty-two, and sixty-four pages. These are Smyth-sewn together to be bound into a book. So when the sheet is cut for you, you've bought it. Also, as I understand it, those pages are intermingled and cannot be separated. In preparing this book for the manufacturer, we have agreed on a total of 176 pages, which for the approximate size required for this work will let the signatures come out even.

When one enters a new vocational community, he doesn't design the rules; he learns them. According to traditional protocol, there is a right way to structure a book, such as always beginning a chapter or other important entry on the right-hand page of the open book, called "recto," and not the left-hand side "verso," even if a blank page is required. Another rule is that the first page of a book is to carry the half title (for what reason I have not the slightest idea), the back of which is skipped for the third page where the title, subtitle, author, and publisher are printed. The fourth page is the copyright page, where the ISBN and Library of Congress Card numbers go. Then other front matter, e.g., table of contents, foreword (not "forward"), dedication, acknowledgments, preface, introduction follow, with the introduction always the last thing before the beginning of the book's text.

May these suggested rules be broken? Certainly--and they are. But I feel in order to impress **some** people with my professionalism, or my desire to attain it, it would be better for me in this instance to follow the crowd. Presently, I am a tyro, eager to leave the fledgling stage and graduate to the status of proficiency.

PLACES TO GO

The writing/publishing family is like that of any other organization--it likes to mix and mingle with the like-minded. There are conventions, book fairs, conferences, seminars, and various other opportunities to learn and meet interesting and helpful people.

The largest annual convention in the USA is the American Booksellers Convention each June in Chicago. Another popular one is the American Library Association, which met in New York this year. Then there is the annual meeting in various places of the Christian Booksellers Convention in America, and many others.

There are book fairs all over the United States and abroad, but the granddaddy of 'em all is the six-day grand finale each October at Frankfurt, Germany. Ann and I are *dreaming* of attending in '97.

BAC'S FUTURE

The future for BAC Publications looks bright. I am steadily gaining expertise and a measure of financial strength, and word of my existence and work is getting around. For example: Four prospects are currently considering me for doing the work on books they plan to self-publish, which brings up a timely subject. Some of our best known authors now started that way. I have a list of twenty before me; I will name eight: Mark Twain, Zane Grey, Upton Sinclair, Carl Sandburg, George Bernard Shaw, Edgar Allen Poe, Rudyard Kipling, and Richard Nixon.

It is almost impossible for the unknown, no matter how worthy, to interest the large publishing house for its eight to fifteen percent royalty. The large publisher is mainly in the business to make money, not to render a service, and must sell 12,000 copies of a book just to recoup its investment. For that reason, "the big boys" favor the celebrity, who can guarantee the sale of that many, or more, books.

It seems to me that those of us who want to write and publish that writing should begin by self-publishing in an effort to establish ourselves, thereby attracting one of the large publishing houses, out of a group of 100--if that is the route we want ultimately to travel. But for now, publishers like BAC Publications can be a godsend in helping the desiring writer get started.

WHY?

Why would I, after retiring from forty-five years of pastoring churches, tackle another profession as difficult as that of writing/publishing?

Throughout those pastoral years, I was attracted to book publishing; yet I felt there was no way I could do it then. Either one--pastoring or publishing--is a full-time job. Although others like W. A. Criswell, Charles Stanley, and

159

Max Lucado have done both, they were/are in bigger situations that afforded more appeal to the large publishing houses and these writers also had valuable and ample staff help that gave them the extra time to publish. So my longtime desire was to attempt the writing/publishing challenge in retirement.

Another reason for my retirement involvement is to continue a ministry unto God, and not live out my remaining years in a vacuum. I publish from a conviction that I personally can produce worthwhile reading while also helping other worthy ones in telling their story.

But my strongest motivation is to share God-taught truth with peers, even recording it for posterity.

THE FORTUNATE ONE

Yes, I've had my ups and downs (and you say, "Welcome to the club!"), but I am thankful to God for the life I've had. By the way, taking the life of Jesus (God in flesh) as an example, there is no way one can live for Him without running, headlong, into trouble. As he lives his life according to the Bible, he will anger the devil and his devotees. Yet what is more wonderful than being born-again, which gives one a spiritual heart able to discern and enjoy that of the Spirit. **What a void in a life that doesn't have it.** And since death is inevitable and inescapable, what is more to be desired than to have the assurance in one's heart that he really belongs to God and that heaven will be his eternal home! It makes sense to me in saying that such is the most marvelous thing (and hope) in all the world.

INDEX

INDEX